THE SHOW

that

NEVER ENDS

Celebrating 40 years of the
York Model Railway Show

by

Mike Cook

Santona Publications
Hull
2002

The Show that Never Ends

First Published in 2002

British Library Cataloguing-in-Publication Data.
A catalogue record for this book is available from the British Library.

First Published in 2002 by;
Santona Publications, Hull.

Printed by The Amadeus Press, West Yorkshire.

ISBN 0 9538448 3 8

The Show that Never Ends

Contents

Foreword

In writing this book I am immediately aware of all those who have, for many years, supported my efforts. I realise that, over the past decade, there has been, and still is, vital support from many who now call themselves "The Friends of South Devon" and to whom, with my advancing years, I look to more and more to undertake the active tasks which I now find increasingly difficult. There are however, individuals who have supported me for well over thirty years - I think of Ben Wood and David Eastoe - the Show Electricians, Gareth Coles who first joined in as a junior, Joe Wills on the 'Treasury' side, Dick Dring doing stewards rostering and keeping exhibitors and stewards on an even keel with an ever available supply of tea and coffee. I think of Ray Wardell and his daughter, Judith, and the many years they ran the door stewarding. I remember those who are no longer with us - Bernard Richmond and his 'man-sized Meccano' barriers, always complaining of my elastic tape measure and supported by my friend John Lundie. I remember Fiona Ellis (nee Banfield) who, until we moved to the Racecourse, held sway with Dick Dring on the Refreshment Bar - who could ever forget her pie and mushy peas! I think of those who can now give less time than they used to - Baz Ward, Ron Willits and Mike Coupland. Then there are those who supported us as teenagers, left to do their own 'thing' but eventually returned, like John Shaw our present treasurer. I look further back and realise how much support I had from my own family in the initial years.

I look on them all as personal friends and know that the Show, which has been and still is a major part of my life, would have been nothing without their support. That is why I dedicate the following to them.

Mike Cook
December 2001

Introduction

I think that if you are to understand how, and why, the York Model Railway Show works, you will need to have some background information about myself. You see, having poured so much of my life into the Show over the years, both it and I have become synonymous, indeed, inseparable.

I hope therefore, that you don't mind me recounting my background at the very beginning of this volume, I feel it is a key factor as to why the York Model Railway Show has been a successful survivor for the last forty years. So here goes...

I was born at the seaside! Yes, in Scarborough to be exact, in 1932. My mother's side of the family were Scarborians and were connected with the railways. My uncle and cousin were both Top Link drivers with the L.N.E.R. and later B.R., although they moved to York long before I did. Uncle Jim (Carry) and cousin Kenny were both based at York M.P.D. whilst I was still in my childhood. I remember well, once going to visit my Aunt Ada and Uncle Jim in Gale Lane, Acomb and being offered a trip to the M.P.D. as my uncle had to collect his wages. I turned the offer down, opting, instead, to play with Kenny's train set! However, let's return to the very beginning of my tale.

My maternal grandmother (my nanna) had been one of the Jowsey family who lived in a railway cottage off Seamer Road in Scarborough. She often told me about her childhood and how she was one of fifteen children. I still wonder to this day how all those kids had been brought up in a two-up, two-down railway cottage!

It had also been the railway which had brought my mother and father together. Father's family were country folk, my paternal grandmother, who had been brought up on a farm near Marishes as one of seventeen children, and my grandfather (who I never knew, as he died of cancer when I was a baby) lived in Dale End, Kirbymoorside (before the town's name got the other 'K'). My father, at that time, worked with horses as a carter and, as such, managed to get a job with the L.N.E.R. in Scarborough, leading goods to and from the depot. My nanna, having fallen upon hard times because of the accidental death of my grandfather, had started to take in lodgers and, as my father needed somewhere to stay, he became one. Needless to say, this is how he met my mother and the eventual result (after marriage, of course) was me!

His job in Scarborough didn't last though and by the time of my birth in 1932, he had returned to Kirby with my mother and had taken a job as a milkman on the farm of Arthur Cousins. This meant he was up and off to work long before I awoke, and he didn't finish at the farm until bed-time either. Thus it was that I was brought up by my mother, rather than my father, and her interests were the ones which influenced me more.

I won't dwell too much upon my childhood. My nanna, in Scarborough, remarried - to John Lund, another of her lodgers and an ex-employee of the railway. He had been 'relieved of his duties' after he had been caught taking bets from some of the station staff! As he was job-less he set up, with his younger brother, as a bookie in his own right and made rather a success of it. Several tales come to mind but as they really have nothing to do with this story I will hold off telling you them now - ask me some other time if you really want to know!

My mother used to take me for the whole of every holiday to Scarborough. Of course we travelled by train, changing at Pickering. Memories of travel in Sentinel steam railcars and push-pull trains are still most vivid. We never went anywhere else - in fact it wasn't until I reached the age of twelve that a different location for a holiday was chosen (it was London) and then only for three days. I loved Scarborough and knew the folk in Gladstone Street as well, if not better, than the folk in Vivers Place in Kirbymoorside!

I became a teenager just after the Second World War, when things were trying to 'get back to normal'. One of the activities starting up again was amateur dramatics. Despite radio and the weekly trip to the cinema, folk tended to make more of their own entertainment than they do today and, if you did 'put on a play' you could be sure of a large, attentive audience (even if some of them did go hoping to see the actors making fools of themselves!). The Kirbymoorside Amateur Dramatic Society was short of male members. I was tempted and offered, and, despite being a little too young, was eventually accepted for a part as juvenile lead in Ian Hay's 'The Sport of Kings'. A reasonable performance must have been staged, for I received good reviews in the local paper. The only thing was, that when it came to the next production, Priestley's 'When We are Married', they didn't call me! I was very, very upset.

By this time my dad had left the milk business and had gone to work with B.A.T.A. Eventually though, the chap whose job he had taken returned from the services and dad had to find another job. This time as porter signalman on the railway. After a short time at Kirby he moved to Nawton Station - the next station along the line. The 'Country Players' at Nawton were short of male members and I was encouraged to join them playing an adult part in Greenwood's 'The Cure for Love'. I stayed with them for several more productions before School Certificate and G.C.E. Advanced Levels claimed most of my time.

Dramatic productions at my school, Lady Lumley's Grammar School at Pickering (by the way, I used to travel daily to school by train), also captivated my attention and the school regularly used to enter me in the speech and verse speaking classes at the Eskdale Tournament of Song in Whitby. In 1951 I won the cup for the entry with the highest mark in all the classes in the Festival and this was reported, together with my photograph in all the local newspapers. By now, I was hooked on a career in drama and, encouraged by my teacher Miss Lawrence, I applied for entry to the Royal Academy of Dramatic Art. As my family were not well off they couldn't afford to send me to R.A.D.A. for two to three years without a scholarship of some kind, so I applied for everything that could be found. Leaving school in the summer of 1951 (after playing Prince Albert in the school's Festival Pageant) and before National Service, I went to R.A.D.A. for an audition. Imagine my disappointment when I was told that I couldn't be accepted for scholarships two years before they were needed. It was possible, though, for me to return for another audition in two years time, after National Service, without paying another application fee. This was encouraging, so I set my mind on doing that.

However, my parents, worried by their perception of the precariousness of the acting profession, started to 'work' on me and, after many hours of argument, they eventually persuaded me that, if I was good enough, I would be 'discovered' anyway, and that it would be much better to have something 'to fall back on' in case I failed. "So," they continued, "why not train for a sound profession such as teaching?" To placate them (though I was not really enthusiastic about it), I applied for a place in St. John's Training College in York and was most surprised when I got accepted! Whilst at the college I played Becket in Eliot's 'Murder in the Cathedral' and Gloucester in 'King Lear', the college authorities wouldn't let students play the lead as they said it would detract too much from their studies! Thus, after two years training, a frustrated actor became a teacher at Westfield Junior School in Acomb, York.

Of course, it wasn't long before my acting abilities got me involved in productions with both the Co-op Players and the Settlement Community Players in York. What proved to be more influential at the time, was that one of my fellow teachers - George Hierons - took me along to Carr Youth Club. Here, not only did I became involved with the running of the club but, eventually, became persuaded to run the drama group producing quite a number of plays and musicals.

Despite thorough enjoyment, I have always felt that one of the major 'drawbacks' with dramatic productions was that you put a terrific amount of effort into them - making of sets, costumes, properties, etc., as well as either producing or acting in them - and, within only two or three days, they were gone forever. I only twice experienced the feeling of longevity with a production, this was when we toured; firstly with 'The Cure for Love' when we played the show in most of the local towns and villages, and also when, in the forces, we extensively toured a concert party production around many RAF bases and amateur theatres in the London area. Perhaps, by producing lasting scenes on a model railway, I have managed to achieve the longevity that mostly evaded me with the stage productions.

The late George Hierons also involved me in the boys' sports activities at the school where we taught, encouraging my involvement in the running of the sports teams and meeting more of the lads from other age groups in the school. Young lads like to natter of course, and it wasn't long before 'train spotting' appeared on the agenda. During conversations with the lads, either whilst doing dinner duty, going to away matches or supervising in the playground, it emerged that they were not able to go down to the station, or away to loco sheds in other towns, because there was no adult to take them and be responsible for them. As I was unattached, lodging away from home and, to a certain extent, lonely, I decided to help them out. We formed a railway club in the school - The Westfield Railway Club. It met on a Wednesday evening after school, and one or two elder brothers were invited along to the meetings too - one of those elder brothers was a certain Bob Dawson! Shed permits were arranged to get parties of the lads around different engine sheds and I suddenly became very popular! Several photos still exist, taken at the time of these visits, and I remember one of the trips very clearly - it was to several of the sheds in Leeds. Whilst we were planning the visit, one of the lads volunteered the information that there was a Model Railway Exhibition in Leeds Corn Exchange that very weekend. So, during the day we visited Neville Hill, Stourton, Farnley Junction and Copley Hill and decided to end our tour with a visit to that exhibition.

I can't remember much of the exhibition, although there was a large continuously running '0' gauge layout and a '00' gauge layout. A layout which really did stand out though, was a model of 'Conway' in TT, complete with castle and bridge. The main feature was the river area which seemed to be built out of a great big metal tray. In my modelling ignorance, I wondered why it was that they had not put any water into it!

Looking back, this could well have been one of the first seeds of my interest in model railways although I do remember some earlier influences. Whilst doing National Service, I visited the home of Bill Peppiatt, a fellow soldier and still a friend to this day. His home was in Finchley and one of the bedrooms was given over to a large continuous-run 4mm layout. It was very impressive and I was most envious. Earlier still, as a boy, I had an '0' gauge tinplate train set but couldn't add much to it because of the war. In fact, just before the war started (I would only be five or six at the time), I can recall going to 'Potty' Watson's shop in Piercey End in Kirby. Here there were boxes of '0' gauge stock piled up on shelves and I can just remember either 'Potty' himself, or his wife, getting the steps out to bring the boxes down. Not much of my early train set can be recalled, apart from my parachute water tower. This I was forbidden from filling after I made a mess of our best carpet when I tried to 'realistically fill the tanks of the engine'! Later, in early teenage, I was deemed to be 'too old' for the train set and it went to my cousins in Nottingham much to my chagrin. For years after that time, my only concerns with railways were as a means of getting from point A to point B and as employment for my father.

Back at Westfield. Each year in November, the school held a Bring and Buy Sale to raise funds towards the cost of the Christmas festivities and parties. Some of the lads, remembering the Leeds Exhibition, suggested that they could bring along their model railway items, join them all up together and make a 'super big' exhibition layout which they could then charge the public to see. Having asked the Headmaster, he granted us permission and we took over one of the classrooms, the lads brought their track, locos, coaches and wagons and spent a hectic few hours assembling everything. The result had to be seen to be believed; the lines traversed desks and tables via variable gradients but it worked in a fashion and we did have a few folk in. The trouble was it was in an upstairs room and away from the main hall where the rest of the 'Sale' was happening, so it didn't really make much money! Nevertheless... the bug had bitten, an interest in model railways had been spawned and a few weeks afterwards, just before Christmas 1960, on seeing an advert in the local Evening Press offering a quantity of 4mm, 3-rail, model railway equipment for sale at a reasonable price, I went to see it and bought it...

The rest of this story is the history of not only myself and my modelling, but also of the York Model Railway Show.

1

To Begin at the Beginning

In the introduction I recalled that I purchased some second-hand Hornby model railway equipment just before Christmas in 1960. This was to provide the basis for the first layout constructed by 'The Westfield Railway Club' and I quote from a copy of the first programme which I still have in my possession:

> "This railway club was founded in October 1960 at Westfield Junior School and holds regular meetings once a week. The membership is open to all boys who have attended or who do attend Westfield Junior School but, at the moment, the membership is restricted to twenty members. The Club aims at all topics of interest connected with railways and arranges regular visits to railway centres throughout England. At the moment we are looking for a permanent home for our layout and club somewhere in Acomb. Anyone who has a SPARE ROOM or KNOWS OF SOME SUITABLE ACCOM-MODATION, please contact Mr. M. Cook, 123, Askham Lane as soon as possible. We MUST have a home before the end of July."

The reason for the above was plain. We met once a week in the school, some of the lads were former pupils and found it most difficult to attend meetings as we had to be out of the building by the time the cleaners had finished! I had tried for support from the headmaster but had received no encouragement whatsoever. The first layout, built using one of Cyril Freezer's plans as basis, was generally housed at the back of my classroom - it measured 8 feet by 5 feet and had an upper and a lower circuit. It took up too much space, though. I had asked the Head if we could use the empty store behind the stage in the school hall but had been refused and with classes the size they were in those days, things were becoming very difficult. The terminus station extension to that first layout was built during Easter 1961 and this resided in the store room for my classroom - again taking up a lot of space. The wiring was far more complicated than that for the main boards (it was possible to control the working of four locomotives at any one time on the layout when it was fully set up). It's interesting to note that I valued the whole lot at £125.00 at that time! we named it 'West Kroyfield' (an anagram of Westfield and York). The reason we had to have a new home by the end of July was that the lads and I had decided to cut our ties with the school completely. The headmaster was beginning to be extremely awkward and was even threatening eviction! You can see that I didn't really get on well with him.

In the meantime, I had become friendly with Mr Arthur Heppell, co-owner of a shopfitting business in town and the father of two lads in the railway club. As the lads were members of the local Church Scout Group too, the railway club had been encouraged to bring the layout and put it on display at their annual Summer Fayre. This was held on Bachelor Hill just over the road from the school. As usual I 'went to town' over arrangements and got really hauled over the coals on one occasion - not by the headmaster, but by Percy Roberts the Director of Youth Services for York. At that time I was doing a little unpaid work in the Youth Service, mostly in the evenings, and was also in charge of the Youth Tennis Team. On the occasion in question, the team were taking part in a tournament in Yeadon, a suburb of Leeds, and I decided that, as the event was a bit slow and the team seemed to be OK, I would pop down into the city centre to pick up some kits, etc., from King Charles Sports Centre for display at the fayre. It took me far longer than I expected and when I returned I was really in trouble! I didn't stay much longer in the Youth Service (this was my choice though, not the director's, and mostly because my spare time was almost fully occupied with the railway club).

As mentioned above, we felt we had to be out of the school because of the rushed timings of the meetings. During the first year both Bob Dawson and Ron Willits came along to meetings from Beckfield Secondary School and found it most difficult as their school closure time was later than ours and we generally had to be out of Westfield before 5.00 p.m. After the summer holidays this situation would be compounded as quite a number of the members were leaving to go on to secondary education at other schools. Thus, at a stormy meeting it was the members' unanimous decision that we should 'look for a home outside the school'.

This led to a great search which at times seemed as if it would prove completely fruitless. The trouble was that in Acomb, where all the lads lived, there was a real dearth of accommodation available at a reasonable rent. Most of the suitable properties had already been taken for garaging cars. We thought we had struck lucky when the local coal merchant said he could provide space. It was only when we discovered that the members would have to keep their voices to a whisper most of the time, build a wall *and* share the accommodation with two horses, that we declined the offer! I had almost given up when our luck turned.

To Begin at the Beginning

At that time I was lodging in the Acomb area, in fact over the road from the school, and my landlady also looked after the son of a Mrs Leaf during the day whilst Mrs Leaf was at work. It was she who volunteered the information that there might be accommodation at the place where they garaged their car. This property, by the side of Acomb Green, had once been a farm and belonged to the Littlewood family who, at that time, owned the local newsagents business. Most of the ground floors of the outbuildings had been turned over to use as garages, but there were one or two buildings with a second storey, it was worth a try, we thought. Initially Mr Littlewood was reluctant but he eventually allowed us to use an old granary for a very reasonable weekly rent. We had a home at last, and little did we realise then that we would stay there for over forty years!

We moved in during the summer holidays of 1961. The members sought out any old furniture that their parents or grandparents didn't need and made the room habitable - well almost! In all those years we never had any running water and had to carry it from sources some distance away. The enthusiasm of the lads didn't diminish at all and, before long, 'West Kroyfield' was altered beyond all recognition, becoming a permanent feature around three sides of the room. The terminus boards were in the left hand corner - the line going from there to a through junction station at the other end of the room and then along the second long side to a return loop under the branch terminus. It was eventually converted from three-rail to two-rail, but I am jumping on a little.

Now that we were in our own home we could meet as many evenings as we wished and for as long as we liked. Usually meetings began at about 6.45 p.m. and ended at 9.00 p.m. They began by being held on Tuesdays and Thursdays, but ended up by being held on most evenings apart from Sunday. We still made our forays to different loco sheds and stations within a day's travelling distance of York and also regularly visited York Station and Dringhouses yard. We also continued to visit local model railway exhibitions too. We didn't, in that first year, get much involved in exhibiting layouts ourselves, although we were asked to assist at the Midsummer Fayre again and felt honour bound to do so. Unfortunately, it was a fiasco! In the previous year, the main difficulty we had faced was excess heat inside the tent we were using - it ruined good operation and folk didn't visit in great numbers as it was so hot inside. We therefore decided, in 1962 to hold the exhibition in the open air with just canvas screens to keep the 'secrecy', and allow us to take admission charges. You've guessed it - it either rained or drizzled all day and the layouts on Show - mostly the members' own ones - stayed under the tarpaulins.

We didn't do the fayre again for we were beginning to establish our club and I made several friends amongst the members' parents. I remember Arthur Wilson, John Wilson's dad, who was an avid collector of railway ephemera. He once offered me a GWR Hall name and number plate (which he too had been offered and didn't want) for £35 - and I refused! Another father, Clive Pritchard (Malcolm and Ian's dad) became one of my best friends during this period, they were a smashing family. I was also introduced to several other folk including York Stationmaster and a chap who was a traveller for the Beecham Group. He was just starting a railway at home and wanted some help - I think it was Arthur Heppell who I have to thank, once again, for the introduction. We became quite good friends and it was he who introduced me to Reg Short of the Knaresborough Model Shop. He also took me, (I didn't drive in those days), to the Britannia Railway Society Exhibition in Knaresborough. This visit must have had some influence for, a few months after, to raise some funds to carry on modelling, we staged our first full scale model railway exhibition. This was in the Church Hall, Front Street, Acomb on Thursday, Friday and Saturday 27th, 28th and 29th of December 1962. It was, in fact, the first *York Model Railway Show*, but neither the members, myself or anyone else knew it at the time!

On looking at the programme for this exhibition (which was produced by yours truly on a typewriter and duplicator) it seems that most of the exhibits were layouts belonging to the members. At least seven were included together with the club's TT3 layout, a display from the club's '00' layout and a layout which had been constructed in my craft classes at the school. Involvement from outside came with a display of Mr Wilson's signalling equipment and also models by Don Quarry who was a well known local modeller. We included stands from the Talyllyn Railway, Ravenglass and Eskdale Railway, Festiniog Railway, the York City and District S.M.E.E. and British Railways, whilst Reg Short of Knaresborough Model Shop had a sales stand along with Rawlings, our most local model shop from just down the road. On the back page of the guide is a history of the club and on reading it we see;

"We have been in our own clubroom for eighteen months and have, in that time, built up quite a sizeable layout (this layout will be featured in the Railway Modeller magazine in the Autumn of next year).

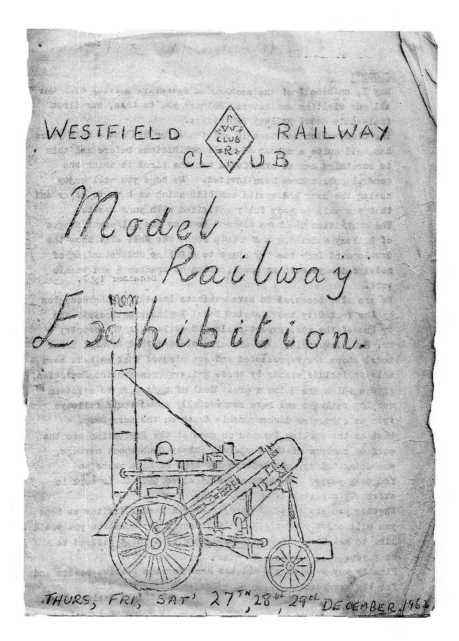

The hand written cover of the first Show Guide. The contents were typed and all the copies were produced on a rotary duplicator.

The Show that Never Ends

We have had many important visitors to see our layout the most recent being Mr C. J. Freezer, the editor of the Railway Modeller Magazine. The club membership has been, for size reasons limited to thirty full members. Their ages range from 9 years to 14 years. It can be truly said that we have never been in any difficulty over membership as whenever a member has left us (which has not happened very often), we have always had at least twenty wanting to take his place and have had a hard job choosing his successor... Trips are generally made every week during the school holiday periods... We hold two meetings a week which are always well attended and try to always have as varied a programme as possible. Finally may I say to all those who have been waiting a long time for membership do not be disheartened as there may be a vacancy some day and, to all our well-wishers and visitors, many thanks for your interest. We hope we have entertained you during your visit to this our first, but we hope, not our last, full-scale exhibition."

Little was I to know...

And on to Better Things!

Things must have happened a short time after the first exhibition. I believe it was the influence of Reg Short initially, and also the Brittania Railway Society, with whom I had begun to be friendly. We were invited to exhibit at their exhibition which was over the August Bank Holiday period and I, as impetuous as ever, decided that we would have to build a 4mm exhibition layout - but of what? All the members felt that it had to be of a prototype. Malcolm and Ian Pritchard had become very active in the club and their dad, Clive, came up with the suggestion of Dawlish - they had often been on holiday there. Just to digress a little, Clive and I had struck up a close friendship and he used to take me out for a drink every Saturday evening. By this time I was living back at my parent's house, in Strensall, as my landlady had been struck down with heart trouble. I remember I rode a motor scooter (a Lambretta) in those days and on one of these Saturday jaunts I left it outside Clive's house only to find, when we returned from the pub, that it had been stolen. The Police found it the next day close by in a ploughed field! Thank goodness, I had forgotten to top up the fuel and the thieves hadn't known how to switch over to the emergency tank.

Anyway, back to Dawlish, Clive said that it was an unusual prototype with a main line for regular services and was very scenic. I had never been there and, on my pay, couldn't see myself going there either, especially if I was to fund another layout! So we sent away for photographs and information from the Tourist Information folk and also wrote to James T. Fraser who, at that time, produced etched name and number plates for 4mm locos and had an address at Dawlish. The tourist people came back with a bit of detail, including a map, whilst Mr Fraser furnished us with a whole collection of photographs. So we went ahead with the planning. But, where to build this portable layout as the clubroom was full of permanent layout and furniture?

The answer came from our landlord who offered to hand over his own garage for the summer and put his car under a lean-to nearby. We had the space, we had the man-power, we had the summer months, including the long summer holiday, so off we set...

All went well and we completed the layout in time for it to be exhibited in Knaresborough at the end of August. We called it 'Lyme Bay', and this is where my seeming love of the G.W.R. started - and see where it's got me today! Of course this appearance led to many other invitations and, before long, there wasn't a school holiday which didn't have us at some exhibition in Yorkshire. What was more important, however, was that we did now have our own 4mm layout for our own exhibitions.

Before the 1962 exhibition I had been in contact with Bob Hunter who, at that time, was clerk in charge of the Railway Museum. I, with my usual cheek, asked if we might loan some smaller artefacts from the Museum. The answer was "Sorry, no," but he did continue, "I have been wanting for quite some time to start a Senior Model Club in York. Would it be possible to produce some leaflets on which the Exhibition would be advertised on one side and I could advertise an inaugural meeting for the club on the other side?" As I saw a cheap means of publicity, I replied, "Yes, of course." Unfortunately, this situation became a little fraught as Bob, in typical fashion, was nowhere to be seen at the exhibition. I had no idea of his ideas apart from the initial question on the handbills so I had to fend off numerous enquiries and point those interested in the direction of the Museum. However, an inaugural meeting was held at the Granby Lodge Hotel, where Bob resided at that time, the society was formed and I became its first secretary, but that is a separate story to be told at some other time.

So, back to our tale with 'Lyme Bay' and its appearances at both Knaresborough and Leeds in 1962.

The clubrooms at Acomb with myself overseeing Newton Abbot Station.

'Lyme Bay' being set up for the Knaresborough show in August 1963.

The influence of those appearances bore greatly upon the make-up of the next exhibition (which, by the way, saw the first use, anywhere, of the word 'Show' instead of 'Exhibition'). This Show was held on January 2nd, 3rd and 4th 1964, again in the Church Hall, Front Street, Acomb. We had become quite friendly with the West Riding members of the T.R.P.S., especially Jim Noble of Leeds and they loaned us printing blocks for pictures in the guide, as did the Railway Modeller. We had met up with Cyril Freezer again at the Leeds Exhibition and he had shown a great interest in our layout. Over the next few years he proved to be a very good friend to the club, as did Jim Noble. We were beginning to become 'known' on the circuit and so were able to invite better quality layouts from much further afield.

The 1964 exhibition included the 'Barnton and Lynstaple and South Wessex Light Railways' from the Britannia Club of Knaresborough, the 'Firthfield Railway' from Sheffield Model Railway Enthusiasts, 'Railway in a TV Set' from Wakefield Railway Modellers and a '000' American layout from Roger Cox of Leeds M.R.S. Two well-known modellers also appeared; Derek Naylor with his narrow gauge 'Aire Valley' and Alan Smith with his 'Lydney Branch' in TT. My favourite story of the Lydney branch is that Alan brought the layout, covered with a polythene sheet, on his car roof rack. The wind was rather turbulent and, when the layout boards were uncovered, it was discovered that a 'great lumberjack in the sky' had chopped down all the trees! Alan had a busy night making more before the exhibition opened on the Saturday. Once again we had support from the preservation movement; The Talyllyn, Festiniog and Ravenglass Societies were joined by the Keighley and Worth Valley in that year. Trade came from Bradford Model Railway Centre. Static Models were provided by Don Quarrie once again plus a large model diesel loco built by Clarksons (D5700) and two models loaned by B.R. - a Lowmac and a bogie bolster. Doug Hutchinson provided three locos from his outdoor layout at Flaxton; an A1 Pacific 'Kenilworth', a J25 goods loco and an LMS 2-6-4 tank loco. David Mitchell (who had become one of my friends through the T.R.P.S.) provided a display of working '0' gauge models on a track situated on the stage. Mr Wilson's railway equipment returned. The York Model Railway Society provided two exhibits - a continental layout from Bob Hunter and a '000' gauge layout built around a toilet seat called 'The Po Valley Railway'. The York club also had a stand on which they gave demonstrations of automatic couplings and sold railway photographs. The Silvermills Club of Otley made the first of many appearances putting on a display of models together with a demonstration from Bruce Clark with his 7mm scale working Cowans Sheldon 36T Breakdown Crane. Our contributions to this second exhibition were threefold; we had 'Lyme Bay', our TT3 layout 'Fizzwell and Little Popping' and also a club stall at which visitors could obtain raffle tickets, magazines and information. The stand also had the Christmas Tree layout where a fully illuminated tree was encircled by two circuits of track - one of which had 'Rocket' and two coaches, and the other, a Sheffield and Manchester electric loco and train. Parents and friends provided the meals and refreshments. The programme from which I have obtained all this information was a much classier affair than those of the past. It was part printed and part duplicated, the printing part was done for us by Joe Wilkinson - a contact provided by Bob Hunter. He printed a card cover which was financed by three adverts; one from our newsagents (Hoggards), our DIY suppliers (Wards of Acomb) and the Micklegate and Monk Bar Model Shops, the latter of which had just opened. As already stated photo blocks had been loaned by the Railway Modeller and by the Talyllyn Railway to produce the page of photos which separated the duplicated sheets in the middle.

We must have made an excess of income at that Show, as we went ahead straightway with developments on the 'Lyme Bay' layout. Already the permanent 'Kroyfield Section' layout, in the clubroom, had been dismantled - we didn't keep layouts very long in those days in fact, by the time it appeared in the Railway Modeller as 'Railway of the Month' it was no longer in existence! The decision to dismantle had been forced upon us, not only by the space considerations but also by the fact that, when the track was re-laid as two rail, steel rails had been used; the clubroom has always been known for its dampness and the rails soon assumed a very realistic rust appearance - great looking but no use whatsoever for efficient operation, so it had to go! During the Spring of 1964 we converted the smallish 'Lyme Bay' into an extensive end to end layout and by the time of the Sheffield M.R.E. exhibition at Whitsuntide, we had 'Dawlish' and the storage sidings ready. Only the six feet central baseboard remained from the old layout all others were new and trackwork had been completely re-laid. 'Newton Abbot, complete with M.P.D.' was finished by the end of August in time for the Knaresborough Exhibition where the layout ran in end-to-end form. This layout also appeared at Leeds that year, backing onto Mike Cole's 'Sundown and Sprawling', right down the middle of the Corn Exchange.

And so, on to our third Show, which proved to be the last in Acomb Church Hall.

2

Farewell Acomb - Hello City Centre

The third Show, held over the New Year period 1964/1965 was the last to be held in Acomb Church Hall. The true fact was that we were outgrowing the facilities there and needed a bigger place. That year we went back to a duplicated programme with my drawing of a Castle Class loco on the front. It is interesting to note how many mentions there were of member clubs of the newly formed East Pennines Association of Railway Modellers. There were advertisements for this and also for the York M.R.S. I, by this time, was no longer secretary of the York Model Railway Society, having been 'elevated' to chairman (where I could do less damage I guess!).

Once again exhibits came from all over Yorkshire. Leeds was very well represented both with a return of Roger Cox's '000' American layout and also their club's '00' layout - there were some teenagers involved with this who have stayed the course and are still with us today. Barnsley and District M.R.S. made a first appearance with the 'St. Ives Branch' in TT3 whilst the 'South Wessex Light Railway' returned from Knaresborough. Another exhibit from Knaresborough was a display from Geoff Mawson's 'Bath Central Railway'. This was a big, permanent layout which our club had visited. Sheffield M.R.E. had two exhibits; Eric and Steve Burdett's 'Ughill and Brookside' and 'Firthfield' in TT3, whilst Wakefield R.M.S. exhibited their '000' layout.

York Society showed their new '00' layout and one of their members, David Elliott, brought a narrow gauge layout, 'Isle of Arken'. Silvermills club from Otley returned with Johnny Robinson's 'Washburn Valley Light Railway' and some static models. Further static models came from the Tees-side S.M.E.E. and Sheffield Model Railway Society. Peter Wright, from Doncaster, exhibited his 'Peterstown Tramway' whilst D.R. Daines of Nottingham showed a fully automatic layout.

One of the features, this year, was a static display of photographs and models mounted by the LMS Society and David Jenkinson. David had just had his 'Marthwaite' layout published as Railway of the Month in the Railway Modeller and he promised me that, if it won the Railway Modeller Cup he would bring it to our next year's Show, despite it being a permanent layout. This led to some interesting weekends later when I had to go along to RAF Linton on Ouse to assist David with the 'conversion' to a portable layout. The Talyllyn put on a special display at this Show to celebrate their centenary and were accompanied by the Ravenglass and Eskdale R.P.S. and Scottish Railway Preservation Societies.

Our contribution at the third Show was the complete new 'South Devon', which stretched down one side of the hall. What is notable is that we were no longer the Westfield Railway Club but had, during the year, changed our name to 'The Castle Railway Circle' (after the locomotive class, not a local historic monument). Thus, we had finally cut off all ties with the old school. Trade was represented by M & R from Leeds and, for the first time, G. N. Slater. George was to become a regular at all our Shows until his retirement and many stories are remembered about this friendly chap who did so much for the model railway hobby. One tale took place a year or two after this Show when we were down in the City Centre. George was staying at the Granby Lodge Hotel and had come out to his car to travel to the Show. He'd placed his briefcase on the top of the car whilst he got in - and left it there. He didn't remember where it had been put until he passed the Odeon cinema about a mile along the route - on stopping he was most surprised to find it was still on the roof!

The year between our Shows again saw us at various towns and cities in Yorkshire exhibiting the club layout. August Bank Holiday was always at the Grammar School in Knaresborough, half term in October was always at Leeds Corn Exchange (where we had experienced model railway exhibitions for the first time). We didn't usually exhibit at Christmas, unless our own Show was being held then, for in 1966 we changed the timing to the February half term holiday. Easter was usually the time of the Ravenglass and Eskdale exhibition at Harrogate and the Whit holiday saw the Sheffield Enthusiasts exhibition in the Cutlers Hall. We also managed to rebuild layouts, add extensions and start new projects - no wonder I was never at home! The truth was that I went straight to the clubroom from school, I often had my tea there, or went to my friend John Hanson's just down the road where I could to go to the toilet if need be, since we had no toilet facilities at the clubroom. Often my visits to John's home would take most of the time and I was frequently supplied with refreshment. The lads began to arrive at approx. 6.30 p.m. and we usually ended the evening at about 9.00 p.m.

I went to live back at home just after we moved into the clubroom and as this was in Strensall, some twelve miles away, initially I travelled by public transport. Later, when I moved schools, I began to use a bicycle but, in any event, there were precious few evenings when I arrived at Strensall before 9.30 p.m. Weekends were not a great deal different:

Farewell Acomb - Hello City Centre

Saturday I worked for a time at the local model shop and, on those occasions when I did that, I went straight to the clubroom when the shop closed. Otherwise, I used to leave home about five thirty in the evening, either on the bus or on my cycle, although generally, it was on the bus as it was usual for grown-up, former club members to visit on a Saturday to see how we were getting on. One visitor, Ron Willits, was a regular and afterwards we often went for a drink in town, followed by a visit to a local night-club, Ron later taking me home in his car. I didn't usually go up to the clubrooms on Sundays unless we had arranged a running session, although occasionally, I did drop in on my own without letting the lads know when there was something special I wanted to do without being interrupted!

Mention was made of the end-to-end version of the 4mm layout and its appearance in the 1965 Show. We found this form to be unmanageable, the trouble was that the clubroom was only about 23 feet in length and it was impossible to set the layout up in its entirety for testing. By this time, as I have already mentioned, the permanent layout in the clubroom had been dismantled and we decided to convert the South Devon layout into a looped eight format. At that time my father, working as signalman at Strensall Station had, with the other signalman, bought the redundant timber buildings on the platforms. B.R., in its wisdom, had decided to close the station to all but goods traffic and demolish the platforms - they offered the buildings at a very cheap price as long as they were taken down. The opportunity was there and I purchased enough timber to build the sub-frame for the South Devon layout. I had been most impressed, when exhibiting at Sheffield, with the idea of layout sub-frames as built by Ken Ball and the chaps from Macclesfield and I thought this could be the best way forward for our layout. The larger legs were built from upright support posts, the lighter and wider horizontal support pieces were of tongue and grooved boards from the walls. It was a good idea but ... it took a long time to erect.

The great advantage was that it could be constructed and made fully level before any of the actual baseboards were placed on it. This was a godsend with our layout, as we had inclines at both ends. I believe that, in the early days, this was our most successful layout. The scenery on it may not have been the best effort, but it did work and something was always moving, though operationally, it did need 100% concentration. The layout featured as Railway of the Month in the February 1966 edition of Railway Modeller. 'Dawlish' ran down one long side of the layout and 'Newton

Abbot' down the other. There was a slight incline from Newton to Dawlish at one end (plus tunnels) and a cross-over section at the other end. The storage sidings were in the centre of the layout from which tracks climbed another incline behind the 'Newton' boards to attain the necessary height to enter the east end of 'Dawlish'. A detail to note at this time was that the motive power fleet on the layout had risen to some 45 locomotives - and was still rising! Also, the branch line terminus, based on Ashburton, had still to be built.

The 1966 Show was held in the Museum Rooms, Museum Street, York - within sight of York Minster and opposite the Public Library. We changed the dates to the February half term holiday, 17th, 18th and 19th to be precise, as we felt it was best to try and miss the possibility of bad mid-winter weather. The Show Guide for that year is a fully printed affair, very like the Leeds exhibition guides. This was because Jim Noble had taken over much of the production side, including the procuring of adverts and so forth. Jim was an active member of the Talyllyn Railway, as was David Mitchell, whose photo of Pendennis Castle graced the cover of the Guide. Because of these contacts we were regularly invited to take part in exhibitions organised by the Talyllyn Area Group - we always attended at our own expense, usually with our smaller layouts and had lots of fun at what were generally one day events at places such as Pudsey and Ilkley. We also, during this period, organised the first club holiday - to Towyn - where we helped out on the Railway and spent time on the beach and in the mountains.

The 1966 Show was the very first Show that David Jenkinson's 'Marthwaite' attended and this fact brought a good number of interested modellers through the doors. Also on Show was our own new version of 'South Devon' still missing the branch terminus, a much extended 'Lydney' from Alan Smith and a return of the 'Washburn Valley Light Railway' from the Silvermills Club of Otley. Two layouts travelled from Sheffield; 'Sheffield Midland and Bolsover' from the Model Railway Enthusiasts and the 'Indian River Railroad' from Eric Slater one of their members. York Model Railway Society TT group brought their 'Regworth and Richill Branch' and Peter Wright returned with his 'Peterstown Tramway'. Another layout from Doncaster was to return in many forms over the years; 'The Far Twittering and Oysterperch' by Eric Fox based on the drawings of Emmet. Harrogate Society brought a 00 layout and there were also static exhibits from the Tees-side S.M.E.E. and York S.M.E.E. The Ravenglass and Eskdale and the Scottish Railway Preservation Societies were also

The whimsical 'Far Twittering and Oysterperch' layout was originally constructed by Eric Fox and made its very first appearance at the York Show in 1966. The railway was recreated several times, including this version by myself which appeared at York in the early 1970s. (Photo: Brian Monaghan)

represented, whilst Geo. Slater, our local Pickerings of Minster Gates, The Model Railway (Mfg) Co., of Kings Cross and Harold Elliott's book stall represented the trade.

A narrow gauge section was also included, 'Michael's Castle Railway', built by ourselves and based on Towyn Pendre but using Isle of Man and other railways' stock. Leeds M.R.S. showed their junior layout which was under the guidance of Jim Noble. Exhibition Officials included myself as Manager, Mrs. Eggleton (one of the parents) as Catering Manager, my mother, Mrs. A. E. Cook, as Door and Programme Sales and Jim Noble as Printing Liaison. I think it was this Show where, for the first time, my father told members of the York S.M.E.E. some 'home truths' about the finances and how much I had put into the club and Show myself, and how little return there was. He then put his foot down and refused to let my mother work on the door again as it made her ill afterwards. In hindsight, I now realise that he was completely right.

Ten months or so later and the 1967 Show saw us back to the New Year period due, if I remember rightly, to the fact that the authorities would not allow time off at half term. We were also back to a duplicated programme, I believe this was because the one we had the year before had cost too much to produce, despite the number of adverts included - isn't it funny how these type of problems often re-occur years later! I also believe this was the time that Jim Noble started to take a back seat. Club members' names appeared in the Guide for the first time too, and it is interesting to look back and see that very few, if any, of the ones who founded the club were still members. There were a few dedicated 'stayers' though, and these formed the backbone of the club for many years, in fact, this was one of the most stable periods in the club's history. We had the help from one of my fellow teachers - Chris Jervis, and many friends and parents took responsibility for barriers whilst certain members took charge of specific layouts. The barriers during this period utilised scaffolding tube and connectors and were hired from Raylors, one of the local suppliers. Although I always asked for clean scaffolding, it was not always sent and more often than not we had to go round with wet cloths to clean the worst of the dirt off. It was also very noisy stuff when it was hastily dismantled after a Show!

The 1967 Guide started a new trend, and one which we have tried to maintain as far as possible in subsequent years; that was as a 'conducted tour'. Layouts on Show were 'Washburn Valley' together with the working breakdown crane, 'South Devon' now complete with the new branch terminus, 'Regworth and Richill', 'Marthwaite' again, with a static display from the LMS Society, and the 'The Far Twittering and Oysterperch'. Several new ones not seen before appeared too, including Dave Howsam's 'Porthleven', Jack Dugdale's wonderful 'Ortogo', Trevor Hughes' 'Trawsfynydd' (this was the first of many appearances at York that Trevor would make over the years) and the wonderful 'Welsh International Railways' of the late Des Welsh from Sheffield. There were also static displays from Macclesfield, Wakefield and Leeds whilst the Scottish R.P.S. and the Talyllyn both had layouts supporting their stands, the latter being built by David Mitchell. The usual traders returned again; Pickerings, G. N. Slater and Harold Elliott.

Things, however, were not going too well in my life during 1967. Events started OK - with the Show, and later, at school with a cup-winning football team (made up of mostly Circle members!). The fact was, I was far from happy at Westfield and didn't really get on with the headmaster. What's more he didn't get on with me, seemingly, he favoured lady teachers far more than men teachers (but that's another story!).

As I said we had a cup-winning football team and, as with the club several years before, they and I didn't want to terminate events just because they were going on to secondary education, so we decided to form a football club outside the school. At the same time the head, at last acknowledging my contribution to the life and fortunes of the school, awarded me a graded post! Giving with one hand, though, he took away with the other: Although he knew that I was happiest with the older years of the junior school age, i.e. 3rd and 4th years, he decided to place me in the 1st year with the lowest stream. For this, I knew I was completely unsuitable and, of course, worried about it - so much so that I became ill and was eventually carted off to the doctors by my father and was diagnosed as having anxiety and stress syndrome (big words for a nervous breakdown!). I was away from teaching for over a term. The head was not pleased about this and, instead of posting my pay cheque, tried to get me into the school by withholding it. When the education authorities heard of this there was real trouble and, one evening, after leaving the club, I was accosted by the head on the way to the bus. I was not ready for such a confrontation and he really upset me with false accusations, putting my recovery back several weeks. The outcome was, eventually, that I was asked to go and see the Chief Education Officer who suggested that I move to another school - this I was more than willing to do. I was moved to another part of the city, to another job, at Fishergate School, where I stayed until my eventual retirement.

These events did have some influence upon the Castle Railway Circle and I am most grateful to the members who stuck by me throughout my illness and got me through the worst of it. I had asked the doctor whether I should close the club whilst I was ill and had been told "definitely not," as it would take my mind off things, and this it certainly did. It did mean though, that I was, in the January of that year, in a very different situation to the one I had been in the year before.

The next two annual Shows (1968 and 1969) were run in conjunction with the York Model Railway Society, with which I was still actively involved. Several of my friends took official positions, especially to take pressure off myself. My friend John Hanson became Floor Manager, Derek Baldock, another friend, became Chief Steward, Barrie Green became responsible for barriers and I was deemed to be the electrician! My mother looked after the refreshments.

In the 1968 Show several layouts returned either from the year before or from two years previous. These included; 'Ortogo', 'Lydney Branch', 'Washburn Valley', 'Trawsfynydd', 'Porthleven' and 'Indian River Railroad'. The York Society had their '00' layout whilst we exhibited our 'South Devon Railway Co.' and 'Ebenseebahn' our continental narrow gauge. David Mitchell brought his '0' gauge back and Frank Turner of the S.R.P.S. had his '00' layout alongside the sales stand. Other preservation stands included the T.R.P.S. and the N.Y.M.R.S. Trade saw the return of Geo. Slater, Harold Elliott, Pickerings (with an unusual layout too) and, for the first time, Rail-Road Scenic Exhibitions of Bradford and Highfield Models (including an 'N' gauge layout).

There were photos in the Guide both by Brian Monaghan and myself, and mostly of our layout!

It was during this period that we started club holidays to Devon and stayed in Dawlish. In the first year we stayed at the Hotel Elizabeth which was a real experience. A number of the lads went, together with John Hanson and myself. It was most strange to leave the train on arrival and step onto the platform which we had modelled (although we'd never seen it in reality until then) and then to walk 'into the backscene'! We obviously made a bit of an impact upon the resort as we were persuaded to visit the offices of the Dawlish Gazette - their weekly paper - being

The 'South Devon Railway' played a key role in many of the Shows in the late 1960s and early 1970s. It was rebuilt several times over that period too. One of the later versions of 'Dawlish' is pictured here. (Photo: Brian Monaghan)

28

featured in that Thursday's issue, towards the end of the holiday. This led to a meeting with the Morgan family, who lived just over the road from the hotel and who we befriended in the following years. We followed this visit up by regular holidays in Dawlish or the surrounding area for over a decade and these were some of the best, most enjoyable, holidays I have ever spent.

The Show in 1969 was the first held over the Easter weekend - the weekend upon which we have held the Show every year since then (apart from once, when we were persuaded to move to the late Spring Bank Holiday. A move which was disastrous, but more of that later). The reason for moving was, once again, to make life a little easier. I had been reliably informed, a few months earlier, that the Model Railway Club who, up to that time, had always used the Easter slot, were moving to the August Bank Holiday. We jumped at the chance to take their place, since running the Show at half term, as we had done for several years, had proved more than a little difficult; we needed time beforehand for preparation, and time afterwards to sort everything out, the Easter slot gave us this extra time. Unfortunately, we *did* cause some hard feelings, especially with the Ravenglass and Eskdale R.P.S., who already ran an exhibition at Harrogate over Easter. Happily though, we did prove that we could co-exist and that having two exhibitions in towns fairly close to each other could prove to be a bonus rather than a liability. This also continued to be the case after the Barnsley Model Railway Club took over from the Ravenglass organisation some years later.

Looking at the Show Guide for 1969, it says that we are, once again, in conjunction with the York Model Railway Society, but in the background, this was already becoming a fraught partnership especially as events within the York Society were to lead to an eventual split. I had already relinquished my position on the committee and several more were threatening to stand down.

Thus for several reasons, the 1969 Show was also rather an 'end of term' one. We had decided to retire the 'South Devon' which had been so successful for us over the years, and several other layouts, which had been regular attendees, were being withdrawn from the circuit; these included 'Regworth and Richill', 'Ortogo' and 'Porthleven'. Other exhibits that year included; 'High Granby' from Harrogate, a new 'Far Twittering' from Paul Towers, the 'N' gauge layout from the Manchester Society, the Leeds MRS '00' layout, Vic Hart's 'Solwyn Valley' from Warrington and Tom Spink of Wakefield with his '00' trams. Our 'Ebenseebahn' returned,

The 'South Devon Railway' won a trophy at the Northern Model Railway Exhibition in 1968. Myself and youthful members of the Castle Railway Circle are pictured with celebrity Ronnie Hilton.

One of my photographs, that of 60530 'Sayajirao' leaving York in 1961, was used as the front cover illustration for the 1969 Guide.

'Ebenseebahn', seen here with myself and Steve Malton, was our club's continental narrow gauge layout constructed in the late 1960s.

as did the S.R.P.S., the Silvermills Club with static exhibits and John Bevan with his 'Vale of York' in '0' gauge. Trade included Minster Model Shop, Slaters, Rail-Road Scenics and Highfield. The front cover of our Guide featured what I believe to be the best photo I have ever taken of a steam locomotive; 60530 'Sayajirao' leaving platform 9N in the summer of 1961.

Incidentally, I became the proud owner of my first 8mm cine camera a few months prior to the Show, and so was able to make a record, not only of this Show, but also of the layout. I still have these precious films in my possession, along with the films I took at Dawlish in the 1960s - Westerns, Warships and all!

So, it was with great reluctance that we retired the South Devon and I quote from an article written at the time:

"This layout was a great success with the viewing public. With its variations of trains, at least a dozen could be operated on each of the main lines, and the complicated train movements which were possible at Newton Abbot - the splitting of trains, changing locos etc., plus, of course, the display of all the spare engines on shed, made it an attraction wherever it appeared. There were also scenic features at each end of the whole and it was honoured to be awarded trophies at Sheffield and Harrogate when it appeared. During its existence it travelled widely and also appeared on television but, eventually, it was decided that the layout had been over exposed, the operators were tired of the hard work needed to erect and dismantle it and it was decided to remodel it so that it would fit around the walls of the clubroom as a permanent structure. The plans to make a permanent South Devon did not, however, come to fulfilment. Newton Abbot was put in place and storage loops were placed on the other side of the room, but Dawlish was never coupled in before a reverse of the plans came about..."

Mention was made of a television appearance, and this happened in a curious fashion. Out of the blue, one day, I had a 'phone call from the chief reporter of the local Yorkshire Evening Press - Chris Brayne. He wrote a lead article, from time to time, about some feature or event in the City and he asked if he could come up to the clubroom with a photographer, as he would like to feature us in his 'John Blunt' column. The visit was completed and the article appeared in the newspaper under the title 'Adventure in an Acomb Farm Loft'. A few days afterwards I was contacted by B.B.C., Leeds and the outcome was a visit to the clubroom by the 'Look North' reporter and a cameraman. An interview took place and some excellent footage of the layout was taken which duly appeared on the programme.

So all in all, the South Devon became quite a celebrity and it became very evident, during the redecoration of the clubroom and preparation of both the Emmet Railway and the narrow gauge layout for the Leeds Exhibition, that we missed her. This was later borne out by many comments at the Leeds Exhibition, truly, the layout was really missed. None more so, as I am often told, than by the Exhibition Manager, Don Townsley. The story is, that our placing in the Leeds Corn Exchange each year was because the shape of the layout filled an otherwise awkward space - I hope that wasn't the only reason we were always being invited back!

In retrospect, there was a clear and underlying dissatisfaction with the operational potential of the replacement layouts. Of this we were sure, and so it was that plans for a completely new South Devon were made after the visit to Leeds. The idea was that we should model a number of stations in South Devon and these should be able to either be exhibited on their own, or jointly with other stations. Dawlish was, through sentiment, to be the first to be remodelled and this would be followed by Kingswear, Ashburton and Exeter St. Davids.

But where to start? Firstly, Newton Abbot was ceremoniously destroyed - the large and unwieldy boards being used as basis for a bonfire. The 'Company' as the builders now called themselves, decided that, to maintain interest, Dawlish should be revived first. New storage boards were built and the good parts of the original Dawlish layout were re-used. A new Coryton Cove was constructed and a new scenic section was made for the 'northern' end of the layout. In this form it was exhibited and a start was made on Kingswear. The new Dawlish was rather like the first 'Lyme Bay', except that the length had increased to 20 feet and the standard of display was improved - as was the modelling too! 'Kingswear' was made in such a way that it would attach to the other side of the Dawlish layout, trains gaining access to the branch by a triangular junction off the down main line. This junction made the turning of locomotives possible when the layout was being operated end-to-end, as a terminus to fiddle sidings layout... but, I am jumping too far ahead. The new 'Dawlish' was ready in good time for our next Show in 1970, our club's 10th Anniversary Show and one which held events which were to influence the future far more than we realised at the time.

The Tenth Anniversary Show - February 1970.

Things began very much as in previous Shows. The major 'event' since our last Show had been the split within York Model Railway Society. The Ebor Group of Railway Modellers had been formed from those leaving the York Society and they had set up a clubroom in the crypt of St. Paul's Church beside the Holgate Road 'iron bridge' over the railway to the south of York Station. This group included all my friends and it was to them that we looked for support for the Anniversary Show. They provided the chief steward, Mike Coupland, the chief door steward Joe Wills, the exhibition electrician, Ben Wood and the chief barrier steward, Barrie Green. Several other members were present but were not named in the programme. Some were exhibiting their own layouts (a rule of the Ebor Group was that all layouts would belong to individual members, there would be no group layouts, as this had generated the problem which had caused the major rift with the York Society). Those exhibiting layouts were as follows; John Bevan, 'Vale of York', Ben Wood, 'The Benwood Branch', Jim and Bernard Richmond, 'Wendale & Arneside Branch' and Neil Coultas with

'Swiss Loop Railway'. My move of school had proved fruitful too, as a layout was built in craft classes there - 'Fishersdale' - which was a kind of 'cabinet' type of layout, in fact, to quote from the Guide;

> "Now we have pleasure of offering you a new type of furniture for your sitting room. Instead of watching the telly you can sit and watch the trains go by, and it also provides a place on which to stand your plants, books and ornaments! The layout was built by Mr Cook and members of his craft group at Fishergate Junior School, and is in the newest gauge, 'N'. It features a stone viaduct over a valley and is one of the first layouts to be built specifically for a locomotive - the Peco Jubilee."

The Castle Railway Circle had three layouts on Show, the 'Ebenseebahn' returned and we had the first showing of 'The New South Devon' in our reconstruction of Dawlish. Only two of the original boards remained from the former layout, "everything else having been newly constructed since December, a record, we consider, even for us!" The third layout we had on Show was our build of a layout to take the Emmet stock which we had purchased from Paul Towers. This, if you remember had originally been built by Eric Fox. My write-up for the Guide is, I believe, one of the best pieces of writing I have ever done for a Show Guide, so please excuse me reprinting it here!

> "Lord Twittering here, been pestered again by one of these reporter chappies to tell you about my new railway. Nothing much to tell really. Moved all the stock last September, brought it nearer to my home - Twittering Towers. Line starts up Cloud Cuckoo Valley - don't know where for sure. Comes into view near Oysterperch Station. Trains don't stop there often - only when they run out of steam. P.C. Sharpnose tells me smugglers have been seen recently nearby, haven't seen any myself though, too busy getting Harriet (my car, not the wife) to start.
>
> Far Twittering's the main station. All amenities - refreshment room, loco' shed. Albert Funnel and Fred Firedoor live in Steam Cottage - nice chaps my engine drivers - do a bit of poaching on the side though. Far Twittering's a junction station - line goes to Puddlecome in the Marsh (used to be Puddlecome on the Marsh 'til a gale flooded it - lost a train too that night). My castle's up on the

hill - open Tuesdays and Thursdays - no wild animals, but special cream teas with my great grandfather's ghost. Monument under the castle is Mrs Brooking's Folly - not much use since the accident so my chappies turned it into a water tower thing for the engines.

Nothing much different in the trains - have a crack express now - 'The Flying Customsman'. Drink when you like in the buffet as long as the train's moving. Never seems to get anywhere - seems to come back though. Well, must rush now. Her Ladyship's cooking pheasant for lunch. Have a look round, but one warning - don't frighten the engines - we had one run off last week!"

(Mrs Brooking was a reference to Betty Brooking (otherwise known as Mrs Cooking), the cook at the Great Cliff Hotel at Dawlish who was a real character - we stayed at this hotel for a number of years when visiting Dawlish.)

Visiting layouts in 1970 were as follows; 'Moreton' by Dave Howsam (Sheffield M.R.S.), 'Starborough' by Harrogate M.R.S., 'Ambleside' by Arthur Whitehead (L.M.S. Society), 'Have-A Go!' by Jack Dugdale, 'Burdale from Grimsby M.R.S., Scottish R.P.S. by Frank Turner, 'Picketts Dale and Haigh Moor Light Railway' by B. Haigh (Barnsley and Dist. M.R.S.), 'The Ashover Branch' from Bill Hudson (also of Barnsley and Dist. M.R.S.), 'Ruddings Wood' from P. Cresswell (Normanton M.R.S. - the first layout of a long friendship with the Normanton club), 'Isle of Man' from Ray Clasper (Wakefield R.M.S.) and 'Brunswick' from the Harrogate M.R.S. Silvermills returned with their usual static display and the Talyllyn Railway also returned with a small layout. Trade was in the hands of E & P Barker (successors to Pickerings), Rail-Road Scenic Exhibitions of Bradford, The Turntable of Leeds, Highfield Models, and the East Pennines Association of Railway Modellers also had a stand.

The Guide was a card covered publication to A5 size with a return of David Mitchell's photo of Pendennis Castle on the front. It was produced for us by Wilkinsons Printers as usual. There were fourteen pages of adverts in a total of thirty two pages and quite a number of photos, including some of my own.

The Museum Rooms in Museum Street were not elastic! Year on Year the Show was becoming more and more popular and, at times during the Show overcrowding became inevitable. The thing was we couldn't afford to hire bigger premises. We were in a very difficult situation. About this time York, for the first time, began to look towards the tourist industry and to promote the wonderful assets it had in its historic buildings. Already there were rumblings about what might happen to the old steam locomotive depot, although the idea of the National Railway Museum was still a little into the future. The City Fathers, in their ultimate wisdom, had recently appointed a Director of Tourism, John Brown, to be responsible for the development of tourism in the city and he visited the Show at one of its more busy times. I can clearly remember him being introduced to me in front of our 'Dawlish' layout and recall well his words of, "This situation cannot go on, you need some help, we would like to help you. If you are willing, please contact me after the show and we can arrange a meeting to discuss how the tourism department can help you."

So it was, that after the Show had been packed away, I made arrangements and went to see the director in his basement office in De Grey House. He was most helpful. His first suggestion was that we needed to expand the area of the Show. My reply was that there was nowhere we could expand it. His suggestion was that we expanded into the Assembly Rooms which were joined by a double doorway at a 90 degree angle to the Museum Rooms. I said that we couldn't afford to do this. He replied that the Tourism Department would pay for this until we had established a financial base strong enough to meet the extra cost. Not only that - he promised as much assistance as possible from the department in publicity, mail shots and any other way in which I felt they might help.

This meeting proved to be a significant watershed in the history of the Show and helped us away from the small exhibition base, on which we had survived for the first ten years, to a new, higher profile, national type Show. One which I have been able to develop ever since. I will be forever grateful to John Brown, and his successor Chris Martins, for helping me along the way during those initial years. It was they who suggested the Show's familiar logo which they produced for us and which we continue to use to this very day.

They were true to their word too, they assisted me in every way imaginable until the Show was established. It is indisputable to say the Show would not be the national event it is today had it not been for that timely and fortuitous visit.

3

A Pause for Thought!

1970 and the 10th Show was a watershed in many different ways, some might say to the detriment of the Shows, but I do not agree with that! When one considers what happens when exhibitors attend exhibitions nowadays, and then compares it with what used to happen at the first ten or twelve York Shows, the changes are unbelievable. In transport alone, the exhibitors of today have it easy! They can go along to a Budget or Kennings outlet, or other van rental firm and hire a van for the duration of the Show without any real difficulty - unless they have no driving licence or cannot stump up the hire charges (which are reimbursed by most Show organisers, usually, before the end of the exhibition).

During the first years of the York Show, as with other Shows, there were no van hire firms. One had to depend very much on friends. I can remember hiring removal vans for more than one exhibition - from both Gills Transport and also a local man who ran a removal business - Stan Howgego. My friendship with Arthur Heppell, the parent of two of the club members and a partner in a shopfitting and joinery business in York city centre, was opportune too as we were often able to borrow one of his vans, but thereby hangs a tale: It was at the time of an appearance of the 'South Devon' at the Leeds Model Railway Exhibition in the Corn Exchange. We had the use of Arthur's van to take us to Leeds on the Thursday morning, travelling back to York that evening, by train, as was usual. Each day of the Show we used British Railways, but had arranged with Arthur to have the use of the van on the Sunday morning to bring the layout back. The van was not available on the Saturday evening, as it was on the way back from the continent where they had been building a new shop front. We had, therefore, to have special dispensation from Don Townsley to leave the layout in the Corn Exchange overnight - it had, however, to be collected by noon as the hire of the hall ended then. With my usual 'organisation', I had arranged for the van to pick me up from York Station just after the first bus of the day arrived there from Strensall. The van was then to go to Acomb, where it would pick up the rest of the crew, and thence to Leeds. I arrived by bus on time to find no van. It didn't turn up for the next thirty or so minutes and I began to get more than a little worried. Going to the nearest 'phone box I telephoned Arthur. His reply was that the van driver had just got back to York after a bad crossing in the fog. He had gone home to bed and they had no other driver so we could not have the van!

A Pause for Thought!

There was no argument - there couldn't be, as he was doing it for free! What was I to do? I anxiously tried one or two contacts, but with no luck, and then I remembered Tom Sellars. Tom was a contact I had made through school activities, especially on trips away with the football team. Perhaps he could help or knew of a contact who could. I rang him up - his answer was, "Stay where you are and I will be with you shortly." He was as good as his word and soon he arrived at the station from Dunnington (a village outside the York) and we were on our way.

Fortunately, the lads we were picking up had had the sense to stay where they were, although they too, were more than a little worried. And so it happened that 'Dawlish' and 'Newton Abbot' rode back to York in a 53 seater luxury coach! What was more, Tom accepted nothing for the job - that was, indeed, true friendship. Yes, we begged parents' cars and trailers, travelled in borrowed vans or scrounged lorries, in fact we travelled in any way we could, and it all added to the experience and the excitement of exhibiting. We even used the trains too, and although I never transported a layout by train, I know of those who did!

That wasn't the only change there's been since 1970. In those days it was usual to travel each day to an exhibition, returning home to sleep. This led to one or two problems, such as when trains weren't on time and you didn't get to the hall until after the exhibition had opened. If you were exhibiting too far from home to enable you to commute (and remember, in those days, it wasn't normal for an exhibition to shut at 5.00 p.m. or 6.00 p.m. - usually they went on to 9.00 p.m. or even 10.00 p.m.), you would be put up at the home of one of the members of the organising club. I have a very clear memory of one of my first 'away' sorties to an early Normanton Exhibition when I, and two junior members, were 'billeted' with Bill Eden. He had a heart of gold - but it was a bit rough and ready.

I have stayed with many folk over the years and have always been most grateful of their hospitality. Up to the 1970 Show we had provided very little accommodation, although several members opened up their homes and I well remember an occasion when the Sheffield Enthusiasts exhibited both 'Sheffield Midland & Bolsover' and 'The Welsh International Railways'. Our house at Strensall being full to overflowing - I had to sleep in my downstairs room in an armchair! During the seventies things began to alter and we started to use hotels and guest houses more frequently - but more of this later, though, these days I often chuckle to myself about those exhibiting folk who moan and grumble about their accommodation, who *must* have en-suite facilities - they wouldn't have stood a chance in the early days!

Another aspect of change has been barriers in front of layouts. When we first started we used tubular steel scaffolding which we hired from Raylors - a scaffolding firm in York. When we first went into the Assembly Rooms we had to cut squares of hardboard to go under the base plates so the latter wouldn't mark the polished floor - unfortunately they allowed the barriers to slide though! We continued with the use of this media until we purchased our own 'Maxi Meccano' - Handiangle. This was better but it did take an age to construct. Bernard Richmond was the supremo here with great help, in later years, from John Lundie. Bernard made up panels of set size to make life a little easier - but because of the awkward shape of the Assembly Rooms, the dreaded pillars and variable layout sizes, I always managed either to give him unusual sized areas to construct or got accused of using my 'elastic' tape measure when marking out; so the atmosphere often became a little fraught on setting-up day!

Over the past decade we have been fortunate, through our friendship with Warley M.R.C., to be able to loan their barriers. These are much lighter and easier to erect than ours, being of lightweight timber supported on metal legs. They take next to no time to put in place and to dismantle afterwards. We are really grateful to Warley M.R.C. for allowing us to use them.

Nowadays, we even have to hire tables, this was unknown in the early years as the halls we booked always had a stock of tables and chairs available. The halls sometimes had screens available too and even a public address system - it was almost unknown for us to have to hire the latter.

Publicity too was easier in those days. You could visit any of the local shops and they would be more than willing to display your posters for as long as you liked. Nowadays, if you want them displayed, you have to bribe them with free tickets to keep them displayed for two weeks! I don't want to 'tar everyone with the same brush' though, as we do still have a small number of folk who willingly display our publicity materials and we're most grateful to them for that. Posters and handbills were the only means of publicity in the early days, unless you could afford to advertise either in the local paper or in the model railway press. Today we can get through 25,000 leaflets and 750+ posters without the least bother and this number increases by the year. We have also gained 'Show Supporters' who, through sponsorship, assist us with publicity allowing us to attain heights we would otherwise never have dreamed of reaching. To these we are, again, extremely grateful.

Finally to refreshments, for both visitors and exhibitors. In the early days these were definitely 'home-made'. The members' parents started the system and, after the first few years, my mother and sister took over. I shall always remember the pans with dozens and dozens of eggs (for the egg sandwiches) boiling on the cooker at home and the unusual smell emanating from the kitchen! When my mother had to give up through ill health, my sister carried on for a short time and then Dick Dring's mother took over for a while. Dick then took charge, with help from Fiona Banfield (who later became Fiona Ellis). They continued to run the service until we had to leave the city centre. One of the drawbacks of going to the Racecourse was that we had to accept the catering of the franchisees - York Banqueting. We would rather have continued to do the job ourselves - but it had to be. However, York Banqueting do a good job, especially in visitor catering, though a little on the expensive side I think!

Exhibitors' catering was easy when all our food was home made. Exhibitors were allowed a daily meal allowance to spend as they wished and our folk put on several 'dishes' to satisfy them - I will never forget Fiona's pie and mushy peas!

For the first few years at the Racecourse, we arranged for the franchisees to provide hot lunches for the exhibitors but, as the price escalated, we have had to return to the meal allowance system. Nowadays all we are able to do is to provide our exhibitors with free tea and coffee - more's the pity. But now I must return to my story...

4

Into the Seventies

In chapter two I told of the involvement of the City of York Tourism Department and the assistance we were to receive from this source. 1971 was the first year of their involvement. From official records I see that attendance figures increased by over 3,000, the attendance for 1970 was 8,847 whilst 1971 saw 12,268 visiting the Show. This situation was to be maintained throughout most of the decade until a decline began in the late 1970s.

1971 saw an increase "in the scope and size of the Show," we mounted "what must be one of the largest exhibitions in the country," to quote from publicity material, visiting layouts came from as far afield as Wallasey and Swindon. This trend increased throughout the decade and became one of the main features of the York Show. Most exhibitions in those days invited exhibits from their local areas - it was less expensive to do so, accommodation costs were less, and so on. The down side was that you were more likely to have seen most of the exhibits before, since most layouts 'did the rounds' of their local area, returning to the same exhibitions year on year. My idea was to invite as many exhibits as I was able to afford, which had not previously been seen, or seen rarely, at Yorkshire exhibitions. I felt that by doing this York Show would attract more custom, especially if those exhibits had been featured in the modelling magazines.

So it was, that as well as exhibits such as 'Woodvale' from Sheffield M.R.S. and 'S.N.C.F.' by the Mallinson brothers of Huddersfield, we included 'Dalcross' from A. Pearce of Swindon, Mike Sharman's 'Modern Image 1850' and Jack Dugdale's 'Ortogotoo'.

Of course we still couldn't afford much in the way of overnight accommodation - the heady days of hotel 'take-over' had yet to come - the staff of at least twenty two of the twenty six layouts in the Show travelled home each day after the Show closed.

1971 also saw the first formal involvement of the Railway Modeller magazine with the editor of the time, Cyril Freezer, in charge of the stand. This involvement continues to the present day and we are most grateful for the continued interest and support 'The Modeller' gives to us.

Also there as a trade stand for the first time, and a regular ever since, was the Wakefield Model Railway Centre, whilst several traders who had been before returned again, including Rail-Road Scenic Exhibitions of Bradford and the local E & P Barker's Model Shop.

It is also interesting to note the presence with stands of not only of the

North Yorkshire Moors Railway, but also the Dart Valley Railway Association and Blue Peter Preservation Society whilst the local group of the Gauge 0 Guild also had a presence with a coarse scale layout, 'Gogner'. The Castle Railway Circle's contribution in 1971 was the return of 'Dawlish', but it is interesting to read that, "Section Two is now in the course of construction and should be on show next year."

Names of exhibitors that year, along with those already mentioned are; Grimsby M.R.S., Frank and Brenda Goddard, Peter Middleton of Highfield Models, David Dunwell and Brian Haigh, Normanton M.R.S., John Robinson of Otley (one of our regular supporters until his death), Arthur Whitehead, Bill Hudson, Dave Howsam, Ron Prattley and Ray Clasper, whilst York modellers included Ben Wood, John Bevan, Joe Wills and the late Bernard and Jim Richmond. Finally, for the first time, we had two trophies which were to be awarded annually, the City of York Trophy for the most original layout and the Peco Cup for the most authentic layout and these continued to be awarded until their condition and the changing 'climate' resulted in their withdrawal.

1971 started the decade off so well, but, like all things concerned with the York Show, this was not to last. The 1970s, although an era of increasing attendance, were fraught with difficulties which could not be foreseen, 1972 was no exception!

After all the planning had been done, the Guide printed, and all arrangements made, I was informed by the City of York Estates Department that we would be unable to use part of the Assembly Rooms. It was to be screened off - rot having been discovered in the brickwork. This prevented the use of the Cube Room and half the Large Annexe and I had to reorganise most the exhibits in the Show to accommodate this change. I did so by omitting only one layout - 'Brunswick' from the Harrogate M.R.S., they brought their 'Layout in a bookcase' instead. We also omitted the 'Railway Cinema' which was scheduled to use the Cube Room. Things, however, turned out to be considerably more cramped than had been originally expected.

Despite this, 1972 saw for the first time many of those modellers who have supported us ever since. I see such layout names as 'Yatton Junction' and 'Mid Gwent' appearing, whilst a group who were to support us for several years. The Yorkshire Crummies (local members of the N.M.R.A.), featured two layouts - one by Peter Wright the other by Frank Howard. Bob Jones from Newcastle M.R.S. has an N gauge layout 'Eightoaks', whilst Trevor Hughes returned with 'Rhiwgoch' and David Jenkinson with his new 'Garsdale Road'. Bill Hudson returned with 'Ashover', Alan Smith

with 'The Lydney Branch' and Des Welsh of Sheffield with his 'Welsh International Railways'. Others who had also supported us in the past returned including Dave Dunwell, Alan Thewsey and Alan Cresswell (Normanton R.M.S.), Ian Lucas, Cliff Sheard and John Farline (Wakefield R.M.S.), Sheffield M.R.S., Roy and Don Mallinson, Frank and Brenda Goddard, Grimsby M.R.S., and John Robinson (Otley). Most of the local York-based layouts featured in 1971 returned in 1972 and our contribution was the first modelling of 'Kingswear' which we had been building for over a year.

Traders included Mike and Hilary Sharman for the first time with 'Mike's Models', Bill Stott with 'Nu-Sto' (which later became Nu-Cast), John Brooke with 'Scalespeed' and Simon Goodyear with 'Goodyear Models'. This Show saw a slight increase in attendance figures to 12,636.

The Show in 1973 was influenced greatly by a Rail Weekend organised by the Director of Tourism which took place at the same time. This was 'The Year of the A4', there were rail tours, A4 hauled of course, various displays and the York Show was involved too. The 1973 Guide included several photographs taken by myself of A4s, and other locos, both around York and in London and we had a fine large scale model of an A4 on display.

However, there were problems too in '73, after just two years we had lost the use of the Museum Rooms - I was informed that they had been closed to make way for a prestigious hotel. This, once built, would have not only an underground car park but also a large reception area reached by the large double doors at the end of the Assembly Rooms - in fact the very ones we had used to access the Museum Rooms. Once the hotel was open, we would be able to use these doors to access the new reception area - so all we would have to do is just wait a few years and we would have a much larger exhibition area than we had had in the past. It all sounded promising, however, in the interim we were offered another hall to replace the Museum Rooms, but I felt that, as this hall was some distance from the Assembly Rooms it would be far too difficult to administer. So we lost what I believe was the more suitable of the two areas for the Show, we were left with just the Assembly Rooms - a venue fraught with difficulties - the main one being those bl...y pillars! I attempted to make up for the lost space by using every inch of the Assembly Rooms that I could, exhibits appeared in the entrance hall, in the Ladies' and Gentlemen's Reception Rooms, in the Rotunda and also the Cube Room.

Richard Barrow and myself pose for a publicity shot with the completed model of Kingswear Station. (Photo: Courtesy Yorkshire Evening Press)

In all there were some 23 layouts along with static displays and eight trade stands. Newcomers to the Show in 1973 were 'The Tatham Light Railway' by three junior modellers, including a 12 year old Neil Rushby! The Balderstone family from Great Harwood brought 'Ruritania'. David Jenkinson's two sons (David and Christopher) exhibited their N gauge 'Seatlle and Carliole' and Arthur Whitehead showed 'Grangemoor'. Paul Towers (a friend who was to return many times over the years, with many layouts) exhibited 'Avalon' and Jack Dugdale had 'Pack-a-Way Mark 1 and Mark 2'. My club had three layouts; 'Furniture with a Difference?', Z gauge and the now completed 'Kingswear'. 'Yatton Junction' returned, as did 'Rhiwgoch' and the Crummies. There were also several local layouts. The Castle Railway Circle also donated a cup which was to be awarded to the most entertaining layout. Visitor support in 1973 was a little down, possibly because of the upheaval of the previous year.

1974: The Ebor Group of Railway Modellers which had been formed through a split with the York Model Railway Society (see chapter two), were part of the assisting 'team'. There had been a series of crises in the months before the Show which had caused the Guide to be reduced in size (I believe the printers had been on strike!). This was the year when 'Yatton Junction' was joined by 'Gainsborough Central', Roy Jackson's layout, 'Winton' by John Pomroy of Oxford, and 'Glen Douglas' in EM, one of Ian Futers' legendary circular layouts. This was the year when we took over the Jorvik Hotel in Marygate and many stories are recorded of that tenure, most of them however are unrepeatable in print, but some appear later in chapter five.

Other layouts that year were 'Wald Stadt' by Mike Smith, 'West Mersea' by Roger Kingstone, 'Beeley' by Brian Lee, 'Burdale' by the Grimsby crew, 'Hudson River Railroad' by Bill Hudson, 'Avalon' and 'Mices' by Paul Towers, 'Quinmont' by Barrie Foster of the Crummies and our contributions were The 'Ebenseebahn' our continental narrow gauge layout and the first appearance of 'Totnes'- the layout which proved to be the most successful one we ever constructed.

Just prior to the Show I was contacted by Andrew Crockart of Ulster T.V. who wished to gain permission to film layouts at the Show. The outcome was not only a three part television series; 'The World of Model and Miniature Railways' but also a part work. 'Totnes' appeared in all three parts of the TV series. We were also asked to feature as

'Totnes' was possibly the Castle Railway Circle's finest layout. It appeared several times at York in the 1970s and won the Railway Modeller Cup in 1975.

The Show that Never Ends

'Railway of the Month' in Railway Modeller and were very honoured to do so. We were humbled when awarded the Railway Modeller Cup in 1975 for that feature.

One innovation in 1974 was the opening to Show visitors of the York '0' Gauge Group's headquarters in Vine Street. We couldn't include John Bevan's 'Hobmoor' layout in the Show - it was far too big, so we mounted a static display and encouraged visitors to go along to Vine Street to see it.

Traders in '74 were; 'Scalespeed', Wakefield Model Railway Centre, Slaters Plasticard Ltd., Railway Modeller, Enterprise Books and E. & P. Barker. Attendance figures that year also increased - but only by about 700.

1975 and the 13th Annual Show. For the first time, officially, the Show was in two separate venues - the Assembly Rooms and the York '0' Gauge Group's Clubrooms in Vine Street, inspired in part by the idea from the previous year. The programme states; "The Show is organised by members of the Castle Railway Circle, Ebor Group of Railway Modellers and the York '0' Gauge Group." This had come about because I was beginning to worry about the financial liability, if ever we were not to 'break even'. At the same time I realised I was not 'super-human' and could do with some help over certain aspects of organisation. As it was, in the long term, I was only permanently relieved of the treasurers' job and refreshments organisation, for otherwise, slowly but surely, all the other aspects of organisation returned to me, but, on reflection, I would rather have it that way for I can keep my finger on all the Show organisation and *KNOW* that everything is getting done - because I'm doing it! True to my Yorkshire roots, I guess! I must say though, that the best thing that happened at that time was the appointment of Joe Wills as treasurer, I am most grateful to him for looking after the money side of things so efficiently over the years until his formal 'retirement' in 1999. He is still around though for the new treasurer, John Shaw, to consult as necessary - the same John being a mere teenager in the period I am writing of at the moment.

The 13th Annual Show saw the return of 'Quinmont', 'Winton', 'Wald Stadt' and 'Totnes'. Ian Futers exhibited with 'Saughtree', Bernard Richmond with 'Pine Creek', Mike Sharman with 'Broad Gauge 1850', Bob Pearson from Grimsby with 'Great Western Branch', Sheffield M.R.S. with 'Manor Park', Paul Towers with 'Pendragon' and Alan Smith with his new 'Hatfield Moor Branch' in TT. There were first appearances for Doreen and Andy Andrews with 'Torandor Valley' and the North Gwent Railway Modellers with 'Pontypool Riverside'. David Hey's 'Portrait of Steam' display of paintings had the first of many appearances. Also present were Tony Morris with 'A Yorkshire Dales Village Scene', and, for the first of almost two decades of appearances, the Archbishop's Railway Circle which originated at the local Archbishop Holgate's Grammar School. Trade included Ossett Mouldings along with our usual traders plus the first appearance of the Ebor Group Secondhand Sales Stand - still one of the features of our Shows. In the Vine Street section (reached by a bus service) were 'Hobmoor' together with a demonstration of scenic construction by John Bevan, a layout 'Ryedale II & III' by R. S. Taylor and F. Brown, the Middleton Railway Trust and Rail-Road Scenic Exhibitions display. The idea of having this 'annexe' did not work as well as expected as very few visitors took the opportunity of the bus journey across town. We did, though, increase attendance by approximately 500 folk that year. The Guide that year was the first to be published for us by Oxford Publishing Co. and it was the last produced to A5 format, ever since then we have produced A4 size Guides. This was a much higher quality production with a card cover and glossy paper inside (but it still had several printing errors!). The Show that year featured a layout in P4 for the first time; Jim Lord's 'Woolrow'. Otherwise, it was a return of those who had been with us before, either with the same layouts or with new constructions. These included; Frank Wilkinson, Doreen and Andy Andrews, the Balderstones, Bill Hudson with 'Tideswell', Grimsby M.R.S., Ian Futers with 'Middleton North', North Gwent Railway Modellers, Mike Smith, Mike Sharman, Bernard Richmond, Barry Foster and the Archbishop's Railway Circle. John Bevan had redesigned 'Hobmoor' so that it could be moved into the main Show whilst we exhibited 'Totnes' again together with 'Far Twittering and Oysterperch'. Steff Torres of the Ebor Group put on a display of his many scratchbuilt locomotives and John Bevan at last got to run his Railway Cinema (although he didn't get sell-out audiences!). Trade was much as in past years and we increased attendance by nearly 1000, mainly, I think because the National Railway Museum opened that year too.

The following year an increase in attendance again occurred, this time by almost 500. The Guide that year was the first of several to have original drawings created for us by David Hey, it also included many more photographs and plans of the layouts on Show. Gone were the days when my humble attempts had to suffice! This year saw the welcome return of 'Yatton Junction' and 'Pontypool Riverside'. The Oxford Club returned with 'Rewley Road' and Ian Futers brought 'Longwitton'. York 0 Gauge Group had their layout there again as had Bill Hudson and Mike Smith. Brian Walkington had 'Reichenbach', Bob Denham had 'Springwood' and

The Show that Never Ends

A. Rush 'The Swaveney Branch' in P4. The Grimsby Club returned with 'Beerthorpe' (what else!), Bernard Richmond had 'Pine Creek' and the Archbishop's Railway Circle, 'Holgate and Inverarnan'. Our contributions in 1977 were 'Alpenbahn', a re-hash of the layout built at Fishergate School several years earlier which had been re-laid to continental narrow gauge, and the 'South Devon' complete with Totnes and Ashburton. There were several additions to the trade in that year - our usual traders were joined by C.C.W., Model Manufacturing Co. and M & R Model Railways.

Over the years our attendance figures had been slowly rising and the circulating space available for our visitors had become more and more congested. The situation was compounded by the numerous pillars in the Assembly Rooms which, needs must, always found themselves mostly in the public walkways. I had, of course, been waiting patiently for the 'luxury hotel' to appear, but nothing had happened. Eventually the Museum Rooms were knocked down, after languishing empty for a number of years - how we could have done with that space. In the end, it was decided that the Hotel would not be built after all, but that the kitchens of the Assembly Rooms would be improved and rebuilt immediately behind those doors! The remaining land would be used for shops.

We just *HAD* to have more space, the Vine Street annexe idea hadn't worked, so it was decided that we would expand into the area offered previously at the De Grey Rooms. It would mean more persons for door duty, stewarding and so forth, but it would give us the vital extra space - and thank goodness we did, for in 1978 we had the highest attendance we have ever recorded in all 40 years of the Show - a total of some 15,481 visitors!

Being a new venture I felt I had to take the responsibility for looking after the De Grey Rooms section of the Show. I asked John Bevan to take over responsibility as Chief Steward at the Assembly Rooms. Unfortunately this did not work out particularly well, for although he did the job for four years, an 'us and them' situation began to emerge and a power struggle seemed on the cards! So, within two years I moved back to the Assembly Rooms to take overall control from there. John Bevan moved from Vine Street to Skeldergate, where he set up his own commercial York Model Railway Company. Commercial and voluntary aspects don't mix too well when it comes to organising 'enthusiast' Shows, and although his group continued to be represented on the committee for a number of years afterwards, eventually they left the organisation rather acrimoniously.

Back now to 1978 and our 'bumper' year. But first, let me update you about my personal situation on the run up to that Show. I had moved back to Strensall and had been living back with my parents for quite a number of years. Dad had retired from his job as a railway signalman, although he still did do the early shift occasionally; if they couldn't find anyone else to do it! I returned from the clubroom (which was about 10 miles away) at about 9.00 p.m. one Monday evening in September 1977, my father was sitting, as was his habit, in one of the easy chairs. I recall his words as I came into the room, "Is it THAT time, I must get off to bed. I'm doing the mail train in the morning." It was then that he discovered, on attempting to get out of the chair, he was paralysed down his right side. The family, apart from myself, were booked to go on holiday to the Norfolk Broads the following Saturday. Dad insisted that my mother, sister and her boy friend continue to go and even arranged with the doctor to be hospitalised for the two weeks they were away!

Hospital turned out to be the best thing that could have happened as he didn't leave until the physio's got him moving again. He was never completely well though, and in the following Summer he had another stroke and passed away.

In the Christmas of 1977 my mother was also taken ill and was rushed into hospital where she remained until the following Easter. We were a close family and whilst all this was going on I still had to organise the Show, fulfil earlier promises to exhibit layouts at various exhibitions, run the club, and continue in my school job. A fraught time indeed, to contemplate putting together a bigger exhibition!

For those who may not know, the De Grey Rooms are in a building about a hundred or so yards from the Assembly Rooms, reached by passing the Theatre Royal. The distance is no great problem, but the main difficulty in 1978 was a very busy controlled road junction that had to be crossed. You could wait for what seemed an eternity to get over! At that time the De Grey Rooms was also the home of the Director of Tourism as well as the Tourist Information Centre and there was a real ale bar on the ground floor which some of our exhibitors discovered very quickly! Upstairs was the ballroom which was the room we were able to use. There was also a cocktail bar off this room which, for the first two years, I used as my office before it too had to be used for exhibits! Also at about this time we started Social Evenings for the exhibitors and they were held on the Saturday evening after the Show in the same room.

In the 16th Annual Show I included the following layouts; 'Hobmoor Branch' from York 'O' Gauge Group, 'Somborne' by Derek Mundy.

'Winton' by John Pomroy and 'Rewley Road' by the Oxford M.R.C. returned, as did 'Springwood' by Bob Denham. 'Wylam' by the Newcastle M.R.C., 'Deadwater' by Ian Futers, 'Brookside' by B.E. Twigg, 'Worth Valley Railway' by the Archbishop's Railway Circle, 'Chepstow' by the Cardiff 4mm Group, 'Swaveney' by A. Rush, 'Torandor Valley Railway' by Doreen and Andy Andrews, 'Reichenbach II' by Brian Walkington, 'Pine Creek' by Bernard Richmond, 'Ravendale' by Steff Torres and 'The Port Newydd & Llwyd Railway' by Terry Onslow. These were in the main hall. At the De Grey Rooms we had; 'Burdale' by the Grimsby M.R.S., Malcolm Clarke's 'The Gwynedd Railway', 'Llangurig' by the Pengwerne M.R.G. from Shrewsbury, 'Milkwood' by Dave Rowe and 'Ashburton' from my group. Altogether there were eleven trade stands or displays.

This Show, more than any other, was to profoundly demonstrate the camaraderie which exists between modellers. My mother was well known and dearly remembered by a good number of the exhibitors and, when it was discovered that she was in hospital, a collection was made and Roger Ellis and myself were 'instructed' to visit mum during the Tuesday afternoon 'bearing gifts'. Needless to say I was worried to leave the Show whilst it was open, but I was assured all would be well. I was also more than a little worried as I knew that, after the Show closed, the lads and I had to collect a van, load up the layout we were exhibiting and go and collect 'Totnes' from the clubroom - we were due to leave for the Wales and West of England Exhibition at Bristol very early the next day!

The traffic on the way to the hospital was extremely heavy and when Roger and I finally got there, Mum was most pleased to see us. She accepted the gifts and told me that I was not to worry about her whilst I was away. I remember feeling that I didn't want to leave, but Roger reminded me that one of the busiest times of the Show was imminent - breakdown - and I would be needed there. Looking back, I am pleased that all my friends had encouraged me to go, and that I made the effort, for, on arrival at Bristol the next day, I received news from my sister that Mum had died early that morning. Needless to say, the rest of the exhibition was rather unreal. Even though we beat 'Dewsbury' and won the Bristol Buffer trophy for the best layout in the exhibition, I was unable to Show the lads the kind of enthusiasm I should. Naturally, as I am sure you will appreciate, my thoughts were elsewhere at the time.

1979 and on the programme cover 'The Talisman' stands at platform 9 with an A4 at the head - one of David Hey's best drawings in my view. The list of layouts was as formidable as ever including, for the first time,

'Kenmore' by Peter Fletcher, 'Dowlais Central', 'Chewton Mendip', 'Tamerig Central', Ian Futers' 'Otterburn Branch', 'Penbury', 'Pendragon', 'Castle Rackrent', 'Lyme Regis', 'Mawddwy Road', 'Portmadoc to Dwffws' by Peter Kazer and 'Butcombe Junction'. There were two static displays plus fourteen trade stands. Layouts were coming from further afield too, it was costing the Show more of course, but I was still maintaining my ideals laid down at the start of the seventies. In my 'welcome' in the Guide I commented on the retirement of 'Totnes' after the Show and also made one blunder by saying that we were showing the *WHOLE* of 'Castle Rackrent'. Richard Chown was quick to pick me up on that! The fact was, that only a part was able to be shown in the space allotted! I never realised this until I finally saw the whole of it on Show a few years ago - how big the complete system is! I ended my introduction with these words;

"We hope you will enjoy seeing the excellent modelling created by our exhibitors and that your recollections of the 1979 Show will be happy ones."

And that, I feel, is what York Shows are all about - enjoyment of excellent modelling! It was unfortunate though that the total attendance dropped by 1500 - but I believe those who did come had a real 'feast' that year.

The end of another decade came with the 1980 Show. John Bevan was still chief steward in the Assembly Rooms whilst my friend, Ron Willits, was chief steward in the De Grey Rooms. I was firmly entrenched in my office in the Assembly Rooms (although I had numerous different locations, each year, for my 'office').

Yet again, we were 'hit for six' by the Estates Department for, after the plans were finalised (as they usually are) in the October of the previous year, we learned, in January that space was to be restricted because of urgent necessary repairs to the building. As my notice in the Guide reads;

"Rather than disappoint visitors or exhibitors we have juggled the plans to include all our attractions. Only one exhibit has had to be reduced in size but we apologise for any inconvenience which may occur through 'Bottlenecks' which may occur at busy times during the Show. The stewards will make every effort to make your visit as comfortable as possible but we hope you will realise the grave difficulties we have to overcome this year in presenting the Show to you."

The Show that Never Ends

In my introduction, I wrote regarding one of our layouts' 'coming of age'. This was a reference to the first part of our 'South Devon' which had appeared at the York Show 18 years earlier. It was unfortunate, therefore, that our offering in 1980 couldn't be operated properly, since this was the layout which had to be reduced in size! The new (rebuilt) 'Kingswear' couldn't be exhibited fully because of the loss of space and thus appeared without its storage sidings - a glorified static model! Other layouts which did appear (complete!) were as follows; North Gwent's 'Dowlais Central', Cardiff 4mm Group's 'Dowlais Caeharris' (one of the few occasions that these two layouts appeared together), Mike Sharman's 'Bogsworth Junction', Ian Futers' 'Lochside', 'Llangurig' by the Pengwerne Group, 'Chewton Mendip' by the Butcombe Junction Group, Mike Smith's 'Wald Stadt', 'Kirkton' by the Kirkton Group, 'Glen Doran' by the Archbishop's Railway Circle, 'Reichenbach II' by Brian Walkington, 'Ravendale' by Steff Torres and 'Brent Barrow' from Swindon M.R.C. Over in the De Grey Rooms we had Mike Marsden's 'Bolton Abbey', 'Calver' by Bill Hudson, 'Somborne' by Derek Mundy, 'Gwynedd Railway' by Malcolm Clarke and Dave Pennington's 'Stanmore'. There were six trade/other stands in the De Grey Rooms and fourteen in the Assembly Rooms.

It was amazing, on reflection, that we were allowed to hold the Show at all that year. I often wonder that had we been in the same situation today, we would definitely have been shut down by the Health and Safety boys! As it was, attendance again dropped (perhaps they had heard about the repair works) by over 3,000 to 10,780 - where had the heady days of the mid '60s and '70s gone?

5

Apres Show
(or What the Public Doesn't See)

(When two or three railway modellers do get themselves together of an evening then there is sure to be mayhem...)

As I related earlier, at the beginning of the 1970s most exhibitors returned home at the end of each days exhibiting, very few stayed over, and those who did were generally billeted with one or other of the members' families. I think 1973 was the year which really caused the difference - the fact was that the numbers of overnight accommodation seekers was just beginning to get too big. I have already told of how my own home was inundated with members of Sheffield Model Railway Enthusiasts assisting Des Welsh with his layout. I know that my mother, who was also running the refreshments at that time, had told me afterwards that 'enough was enough'. The next year we had a big influx of visiting layouts from some distance away; 'Yatton', 'Winton' and 'Gainsborough' to name but three, and so I decided that we would have to start booking folk into hotels and guest houses. We received initial support from the tourism office and chose, as one of our hotels, the Jorvik in Marygate. We were to return there for quite a number of years and many of our exhibitors have happy memories, especially of the cellar bar at that hotel!

The Elliotts, who owned the Jorvik, I am sure didn't realise, when they first agreed to our using their facilities, what they were letting themselves in for, but, like the good folk they were, they accepted all that went on and even presented a trophy to be awarded at the Show - I don't know whether they fully appreciated my decision to award it to the exhibitor who had behaved the most outrageously - It seemed apt though. Many are the tales of the Jorvik, some, as I said in chapter four are unprintable but there are others which I can now divulge. I trust the folk I mention by name will take it in the spirit it is meant and not be upset, but this 'Apres Show' aspect, I feel, is equally important to the smooth running of the event, as is everything else.

I have mentioned the cellar bar at the hotel - it wasn't very big and was usually at bursting point every evening - especially after closing time! Mr Elliott always, after the first year, used to get in a stock of Tetley's bitter which generally disappeared with great speed! It was here you met with the 'other side' of peoples' personalities. I well remember Tony Reynalds singing along to his own guitar accompaniment and composing a special

York Show Song which featured other exhibitors' foibles and misdemeanours in its verses. This was only the first of many such compositions over the years. Roger Ellis composed some as did Dave Hackling and even I was known to put pen to paper occasionally. Tetleys must have been singing beer, for the songs came thick and fast until the early hours of the morning. It was not unusual for Mr. Elliott to remark, "You know where the till is and where the beer is - serve yourself, I'm going to bed."

It was in that bar that we, sometimes, had sight of Cyril Freezer's little black notebook. If Cyril found himself in the position of having to buy someone a drink - which did happen occasionally, then out would come the little book to have the amount recorded. We never did find out why but thought perhaps he might be able to claim it back on expenses! Cyril was a good friend to have in those days, as editor of the Railway Modeller, he helped out enormously with publicity for the Show and I don't think I ever saw him in a state of intoxication. More than I can say of his lads though, although his younger son appeared to take his alcohol better than his elder brother who was found, one night, on his knees before the toilet praying vehemently to 'Huey' after a session in the bar! One remembers Derek Mundy playing the newel post as a string bass and I will never forget the final night, one year, when Ian Issitt stayed with us. Ian, at that time, lived in Paignton and was having to drive back to Devon the next morning. He had therefore had a swift drink but retired early to get sufficient rest before the journey. One of his team, returning from the toilet, realised Ian had disappeared before he had had the opportunity to buy him a return drink and went up to Ian's room insisting he returned to the bar. His powers of persuasion must have been tremendous as, with great reluctance, Ian appeared in his dressing gown whereupon he was presented with a pint of beer and instructed to drink it. Ian took the beer - and poured it straight over the said gentleman's head and then returned upstairs without a word!

Amongst the Yatton Junction Group were several police officers and one (for a joke) brought up a breathalyser kit. This he insisted on testing out on Brian Chappell (one of Yatton Group) and Paul Powell (of the Mid Gwent group) the next morning after one of the usual sessions. Of course they were shocked to find that they were still both positive, but this did give them both the excuse for not sharing the driving on the way home! The same Paul Powell (unfortunately now no longer with us) was the perpetrator of many "japes and wheezes" as he used to call them. Passers by in Marygate, one morning, were surprised, nay shocked, to see a lightly

Apres Show. The inimitable Paul Powell (top), perpetrator of many 'japes and wheezes' in a characteristic pose. In contrast, myself and Ron Willits (below) relax in a less exuberant mood after one of the Shows.

clad Powell on the upstairs balcony giving an excellent impression of Adolph Hitler delivering one of his most vehement speeches.

Needless to say these antics couldn't continue forever and, after a few years, I was regretfully informed that the Jorvik was entering into an agreement with Golden Rail which meant that they could no longer allow us to use their facilities. Consequently, I had to find alternative accommodation. It says much for the ambience of the place that, although we never used it after that time, many of the exhibitors returned, year on year, to visit the Elliotts. I had used the Georgian Guest House in Bootham for the overflow for a few years so we initially moved over there as our major spot. The trouble was the Georgian had no bar, so 'celebrations' had to be organised elsewhere, neither was it as big as the Jorvik, and as numbers of exhibitors were increasing each year, we had to use several different hotels and guest houses in the Bootham area.

One Hotel which we used for a short time was the Bootham Bar Hotel - the North Gwent were 'billeted' there. They enjoyed a good pint and as it wasn't licensed premises, they thought it should be called 'The Bootham Non-Bar Hotel'. They told several stories about the place and I have Alastair Warrington to thank for the definitive version of the following: North Gwent had arrived back late one night, I cannot remember where they had been - perhaps to see the Elliotts. Steve Vincent arrived back first and, unfortunately, slammed the door shut causing the latch to drop. The other three could not get in. John Cox decided to wait until the others had found a way in and witnessed little of what was to follow. The other two, Alastair and Paul Powell, being folk of ingenuity (or perhaps it was because they were just intoxicated) decided, instead of ringing the front door bell, to climb the dexion fire escape which ran from the garden of the hotel up to their room. However, to get into the garden, they had first to gain access onto the ancient City Walls. In this, they were lucky, as Bootham Bar itself was encased in scaffolding since it was under repair. Gaining access to the wall however did not assist them greatly as they still had to reach the garden which was a number of feet below. Alastair had the idea of climbing into a nearby tree and climbing down. This he managed to do - unlike Paul - who fell out of the tree! By this time Alastair had scaled the fire escape and reached the bedroom reasonably quietly. Paul on the other hand, had created quite an amount of noise - enough in fact, to wake the proprietors. As he bounded up the fire escape he found himself threatened with a shot gun which, in his inimitable way, he simply brushed aside. When they both finally reached the safety of their bedroom, thinking they had got away with it, there came a load knock on the door. The pair came face-to-face with a very irate landlord with blunderbuss in hand and clothed only in a night-shirt and night-cap - complete with tassel! He demanded to know what was going on and informed them that in all his years in the hotel trade he had never had an experience such as this before. He said that they were to leave next morning and then went back to bed. At this point they remembered John who was still waiting patiently on the front door step, so, extremely quietly, they went and let him in. Luckily the landlord relented next morning, but they were never closer to being thrown out of an hotel because of an escapade than they were that night. As for me, well, I never dared use *that* hotel again.

Of course being in a number of different hotels and guest houses wasn't the same as all being in the same location and, for a few years, on the instigation of John Bevan (whose Model Company used the old sawmill next door), we moved to the Lady Anne Middleton's Hotel in Skeldergate where we were able to let 'celebrations' go on for as long as we liked. Here, I well remember Gareth Coles slowly slipping down the door jamb as he got steadily drunker. Curiously, there was a deep well in the middle of the bar area which was protected with a wooden cover. It is rumoured that it was not unusual for the lid to be removed at some time during the weekend by those not wanting to make the journey to the toilet! Though I can't, of course, vouch for that story.

John Bevan, ever the joker, once brought an inflatable doll - one of the Cardiff Group had a real shock when he woke up with her in bed next to him! The next morning she was discovered as a tree decoration in the hotel conservatory.

The trouble was, that as York became more popular as a tourist centre, hotel charges increased. This occurred with the Lady Anne Middleton's and before long we couldn't afford it any more and had to find alternative accommodation again. We moved back to the Georgian which was now being run by Kathy Holt. For the remainder of our time in the City Centre we continued to use this Guest House, especially as she also took over Evelyn House next door. We also used several other hotels and guest houses in the Bootham area but on moving to the Racecourse, we started to use places nearer to the venue, although we continued to use Evelyn House (which Kathy ran with her son Craig after selling the Georgian Guest House) until 2001 when, unfortunately for us, Kathy sold Evelyn House and retired.

I mentioned, earlier, the official social evenings which really began when we first started to use the De Grey Rooms. These often continued on an ad hoc basis in several of the hostelries of the good City of York. One recalls the evenings we had at the Acorn in St. Martins Lane, the Spread Eagle in Walmgate, The John Bull (now closed), The Brown Cow as well as the De Grey Rooms Bar itself. Several of the regular exhibitors always included the Bootham Tavern in their travels, especially the North Gwent boys who returned, year on year, to play 'Doms' in the Bootham. We also, for a time used the back room at the Wagon and Horses in Gillygate.

I also tried to make the evenings more attractive by arranging trips out to different locations a little way from York. We have visited Sheriff Hutton, Cawood, Easingwold, Ampleforth and Malton amongst others. The arrangement was to organise transport, book a room at a hostelry, provide a light buffet and just let the evening take its course - it usually did! As time went on, though, this type of arrangement became more difficult as the numbers of exhibitors grew and we had to opt for a more formal type of evening. The first venue we used was the English Martyrs Hall where we had a real ale bar, a ceilidh band and a buffet provided by Joe Wills' late wife Irene and her friend. Later we moved the venue when the chap running the hall wanted to provide keg beer - as a real ale fan, I would have none of this of course! We then moved back to the De Grey Rooms where we stayed until 1999 when we made our most recent move to the Merchant Adventurers' Hall.

Well, I have jumped on in time to the present once again, so, to return to the mid seventies: The Show was held at that time on Easter Saturday, Monday and Tuesday. We didn't open on the Sunday. This was initially forced upon us by the authorities but, later, when the regulations were relaxed, our committee members felt that they should continue to have the Sunday off with their families. This did mean that we had a 'dead' day in the middle of the Show. No matter - let's use it to our advantage. So it became a ritual for the exhibitors to take a coach trip (or go in their cars) to the North Yorkshire Moors Railway (once or twice for a change, we went to the Keighley and Worth Valley). This tended to be a late morning to late evening excursion combined with a certain quantity of beer and song. When we started to open the Show on Sundays we had to forgo the whole day excursions but I still arranged an evening trip to the N.Y.M.R. and either Goathland or Whitby. The trips were always enjoyed by all who went on them and they continued until we returned to a three day Show in 2001.

By now you will have gathered that the exhibitors and some of the officials have an enjoyable time, not only at the Show but also at other times over the weekend. This is, as I have already stated, very important as folk give of their own free time to come to the city and work hard to make the York Show a success for all our paying visitors. So, as Show Manager, what I feel we must do, is make their weekend with us as pleasant as possible. What's more, I do believe that the formula has worked well over the years.

I've mentioned 'real ale' several times in this chapter and thereby hangs a tale. In the years before the Shows began, I didn't drink - well only very occasionally. It's funny how model railways and real ale seem to go in partnership - must be to do with preserving the good things in life! It is a well known fact that you have to have a certain amount of stamina to last out a York Show - especially if you go out for a drink each evening. At one time the whole situation started to get more than a little out of hand. My love of real ale, which was shared by several regular exhibitors at the Show, led to those of our friends from further afield bringing real ale with them! The barrels were set up discretely in my office for consumption as and when required. This situation continued for a few years until one year when my 'office' was in the centre of the main layout area in the Assembly Rooms. In there, were 'racked' a barrel of Brains Dark, a barrel of Timothy Taylors Best Bitter, a barrel of Taylor's Landlord and a barrel of Scrumpy! One afternoon during the Show some of the exhibitors decided to use the hall's grand piano (which was stored out of the way in the same area as the 'office') and have a sing-song whilst the Show was still open to the public. Ian Futers (who, by the way, does not drink alcohol) was persuaded to play and was joined, in duet, by Terry Onslow. They were very good but... after this escapade I was taken to task by one of my committee who felt that the situation was really getting out of hand. I saw his point of view and, to a certain extent agreed with him, after all, it was a model railway show and not a beer festival! Since that time we have kept most of our 'celebrations' low key or outside the hours of the Show, we've also become a great deal older and, I hope, wiser.

Over the years I have made many dear friends amongst the exhibitors who have come to the Show. It would be difficult to name them all and I would hate to miss out anyone from such a list. These friendships have led to many holiday visits where I have had most enjoyable times being accepted as a genuine friend in their homes. In fact, I often say, that I have more friends throughout the length and breadth of Great Britain than I have locally. I thank them all for their lasting friendship and for always being on the other end of the 'phone when I need them. I don't know wherever I would be without them.

6

Into the Eighties

Before continuing this 'history', I feel I must give some indication of the attendance since records were first kept in 1969/70. I am not a 'number cruncher' generally but I feel you do need to keep a record of attendance to be able to gauge the popularity of the Show and how well (or badly) you are doing financially. This was a very important influence in the first years as I had no 'back-up' fund in case we lost out - I would have had to sustain any loss from my own pocket which was already greatly stretched with running the club. Luckily I never failed to break even with the Shows but it was a great financial worry - one which led me, eventually, to bring in more folk to bear the burden (if it were necessary). I never, though, allowed control of the Show to leave my grasp and did on one or two occasions, have real battles to keep my hold on the Show, especially when others saw potential 'rich pickings' - as they thought - from being in a position of control. The latter was, in fact, never the case. I never made anything personally from the Show - the only ones to gain from any money made were the club members, where the excess of income paid for equipment, materials and so forth. This is exactly the same situation as with all clubs that put on exhibitions, any excess being ploughed back into the organisation as a way of raising funds. Similarly, and it does happen, the liability for any shortfall coming out of club funds.

Of course, increased club funds also made it a great deal easier for me to live on my earnings from teaching - I didn't have to put so much of my wages into the club!

Anyway back to attendance figures: In 1969 and 1970 attendance was around the 8900 mark. This was at the time of the first involvement of the Tourism Director. The next year it rose over 3,000 and began a steady climb in the following years until it reached a peak in 1978 of over 15,000. These were 'heady' days but also uncomfortable for the visitors and it was during this time that we were accused of being complacent about overcrowding. From 1978 we started to drop - in the first year by 1,000 but then by 3,000 - so we had entered the 1980s around the 10,000 mark. I have already spoken of the 1980 Show in chapter four, the one in 1981 saw us again open on the Saturday, Monday and Tuesday in both the Assembly Rooms and De Grey Rooms. One of the 'feature' layouts that year was Bob Harper's 'Chewton Mendip' and little did I realise at that time that Bob would later become one of my closest friends.

1981

Along with Bob Harper's 'Chewton Mendip', the Cardiff lads brought 'Chepstow'and the Yorkshire Crummies, 'Pateleyville'. Paul Towers' effort that year was 'Pendragon Tramway' whilst Ian Futers brought 'Kielder Forest'. Peter Kazer exhibited 'Dinas Junction' and Roy Jackson 'High Dyke'. The Butcombe Junction Group exhibited 'Chewton Mendip' and Alan Smith returned with 'Hatfield Moor', We exhibited 'Kingswear' and other layouts came from Andy Gibb 'Meadowtown', Frank Wilkinson 'Hundhaus', Terry Onslow 'Trefolwen', Dave Walker 'Laxford Bridge' and the Kirton Group 'West Road'. Trade saw DJH for the first time, the Oxford Publishing Co. (who produced the Guide for us) and Derek Mundy with his Sprat and Winkle Couplings. Others included Railway Modeller, Wakefield Model Railway Centre, M. & R. Models, Mike Sharman Wheels, York Model Co., Jidenco, Slaters, BTA Trees, Scalespeed and Railmail of Watford.

By now the content of each Show was growing ever larger and the exhibit listings on the 'Bill' ever longer. So from here onward, the exhibits of each Show are being listed in separate panels, rather than in the main text. Attendance in 1981 showed a rise of just over 1,000, which was a welcome relief from the previous downturns.

1982 saw our 20th Show again using both the Assembly Rooms and De Grey Rooms and opening on Saturday, Monday and Tuesday. This Show saw the first appearance of a 'Z' gauge layout - 'Inverary' by Paul Towers.

Visitor numbers in 1982 returned to the downward path - just over 11,000 attended that year. So for 1983, I had tried to generate more local interest by organising a York Schools 'Build a Locomotive' competition. Unfortunately, this was not well supported and did not have the success it deserved. Thus, 1983 saw us back in the two halls and on the usual three days, and this year various difficulties prevented the attendance of a couple of special exhibits attending that I had had in mind. Firstly, we had hoped to include the North Devon Group as exhibitors but, unfortunately, they were unable to exhibit 'Penthaven Bridge' because of staffing difficulties and were substituted at very short notice by Alwyn Pulleyn's 'Riccall' in 'N' gauge. Secondly, I had hoped to realise a special wish that was never fulfilled - to have Rev. Wilbur Awdry exhibit one of his layouts at York - in this case 'Ulfstead Road'. Unfortunately he also had to cancel because

1982

As well as 'Inverary' by Paul Towers this Show featured 'Kingsbridge' from Wakefield Modellers; Mike Bradley, Mike Evans and Bob Smith. Nigel McMillan's 'Lyoncrosse Colliery', 'Fordley Park' from Wolverhampton M.R.S. and a certain Dave Peacey with 'Highworth - Hannington'. Dave Walker's 'Laxford Bridge'returned in extended form, John Dunford and Chris Mountain brought 'Southwold Light Railway', the Crummies returned with 'Pateleyville Joint Terminal Railroad'. The Keighley Group of the Gauge '0' Guild exhibited 'Leeds Road'. Local modeller Steff Torres exhibited 'Ravendale' whilst D. Orme showed 'Vale of Rhyngwerm'. Regulars included Cardiff 4mm Group with 'Chepstow', Derek Mundy with 'Sombourne', the Butcombe Junction Group with 'Nempnett Thrubwell' and the North Gwent Railway Modellers with 'Blaenavon'. Local modeller Bob Dawson had 'Beck-in-Dale' whilst Peter Fletcher and the Archbishop's Railway Circle had 'Lawers'. Our club offering this year was 'Ashburton'.

of illness - I never did manage to get him to the York Show. In the De Grey Rooms the Leeds. M.R.S. exhibited a layout which, for me, never reached its true potential before being pensioned off - 'Brent' in '0' gauge. This year attendance dropped by almost two thousand - still, we soldiered on.

1983

This year saw 'Chiltern Green and Luton Hoo' from the Model Railway Club. Barry Norman brought 'Wyndlesham Cove'. Other layouts included our own 'Ashburton', Leeds M.R.S. 'Brent', Paul Towers's 'Futtocks End', Bernard Richmond's 'Gorbern Creek', North Gwent's model of 'Caerleon', Cardiff 4mm Group's 'Narberth', Butcombe Junction Group's 'Nempnett Thrubwell', Terry Onslow's 'Witton', Ian Futers' 'Scotsgap Junction', 'Lawers' by Archbishop's Railway Circle, John Dunford's 'Shire Light Railway', 'Milverton', N. and P. Adams and 'Mellison Bridge' by Keith Foster and Pete Dickenson. In the trade part of the Show George Norton appeared for the first time as did PhotoRail Processing. The Transport Scene replaced the Oxford Publishing Company as our 'Book Shop'. Also featured were Rail-Road Scenics of Bradford, Jidenco, Colin Massingham's MTK, Westdale and Ratio - for the first time.

Into the Eighties

We opened on Easter Saturday, Monday and Tuesday in 1984 still in the Assembly Rooms and De Grey Rooms, but ... there was a wind of change beginning to blow... attendance, this year, collapsed to between six and seven thousand; a great many questions were being asked. This was also the year referred to in chapter five - the year of the beer! It was true, the good days were finally coming to an end and I had to begin watching my back!

However, present in 1984 for the very first time, were a group who have become some of the Shows best friends and supporters; the Warley Model Railway Club with 'Halesowen'. This year too, I ran another competition in the York Area schools - to design a poster for the Show. It had a better support than the previous year's modelling competition, but was still not as well supported as I had hoped.

1984

Returning layouts this year included 'Fordley Park', 'Narberth', 'Caerleon', 'Nempnett Thrubwell' and Bob Dawson's 'Beck-in-Dale'. The contemporary scene was featured on 'Tipple Lane' by Dave Peacey. Others layouts were; Derek Lane's 'Stuart's Lane M.P.D.' Ian Futers' 'Burnfoot'. 'Shapwick' by Jeff Gay and 'Rye Harbour' by the late Martin Brent (Martin became a good friend and supporter of the York Shows over the years until his untimely death). Dick Wyatt brought 'Dovey Valley' for the first time, Adrian Ponting exhibited 'Treacle Bolly', there was 'Peakwell' from Blackburn and District M.R.S. and the 'Shire Light Railway' from John Dunford. The Ebor Group showed 'Low Kyme', Mike Hayward brought 'Chesil Bay', Nigel MacMillan brought 'Campbeltown and Macrihanish', Peter Kazer with 'Welsh Narrow Gauge' and Paul Cope, of the Archbishop's Railway Circle with 'Gilling Railway'. The Warley Model Railway Club attended for the first time with 'Halesowen'. New traders, that year, included ECM Controls and RSB Models of Middlesbrough - Ron Banks continued to attend each year until his eventual retirement from the model trade.

1985 and, as hinted, all change! The Show reverted to the Assembly Rooms only, but became a three-and-a-half day Show. Yes, for the first time we opened from noon to 5.00 p.m. on the Sunday. It was stated, regarding the move to one hall only, that it was "a move forced on us by the financial climate of the present times." This Show seemed to be more of a 4mm exhibition than anything else. We did have one 3mm layout, 'Fraalsdorf'

1985

Layouts on display at the 1985 Show were 'Y Ten Bach' by Malcolm Clarke, 'Leighton Buzzard', Dave Rowe, 'Caerleon' by North Gwent, 'Evercreech Junction' from Shipley M.R.S., 'Highworth - Hannington' by Dave Peacey, 'Gilling Railway' from Paul Cope, 'Glenmore' by Peter Fletcher, 'Roseladden Wharf', Steve Howe, 'Dowlais Cae Harris', Cardiff 4mm Group, 'Petherick' by Barry Norman, 'Bevleys' by Dave and Bev Lowery, 'Ubley'from the Butcombe Junction Group, 'Kyle of Tongue' by Steve Flint and 'Huntingfield' by Keith Foster. My own group also put on a display commemorating GWR 150 and new amongst the traders were Precision Paints.

This year York Show included 'Kyle of Tongue', a 1970s Scottish Region layout depicting a plausible terminus in the Far North.

by Frank Wilkinson, but all others seemed to be in 4mm, some of it was narrow gauge though! This year I utilised every available inch of space in the Assembly Rooms and included sixteen layouts. Despite this, we managed a rise in attendance of just over 1,000.

Between the 23rd and 24th Shows two of our 'regulars' got married. Roger Ellis from Cleethorpes tied the knot with our 'Catering Manageress' Fiona Banfield and many of the exhibitors, from far and wide attended the ceremony in York. Roger and Fiona, with their son Frederick have been staunch supporters of the Show ever since although it has been impossible for them to be as active. It was a great shock to us all when, just before the 39th Show, we learned of Fiona's untimely death. Roger, however, is still very much with us and I hope he will be able to exhibit a layout at the 40th Show.

In the introduction to the 24th Show in the 1986 Guide, I included the following words;

"Over the past few years I have been asked by several visitors why my own layouts, which were featured regularly at Shows up to four or five years ago, have been absent. The reason is simply that I have found it impossible to manage a Show properly and also ensure that a layout worked efficiently throughout the same Show. So it must be that my present layouts; 'Leambury', 'Castle Cary' and 'Ashburton' must always play 'away fixtures'."

I did, however, include seventeen layouts in the Show that year, as listed in the panel below.

1986

Layouts: 'Haigh Town' from Normanton and Pontefract R.M.S., 'Crystal River Railroad' from Roger Nicholls and 'Glengorran and Stededge Junction' from the Ebor Group. 'Saunton Sands and Woolacombe' from John Bateman, 'Llandoug' by Neil and Doug Metcalfe. 'Exeter St. Leonards' from John Brewer. In 00 we had 'Shaunton Minster' from Bristol 4.1.4. Group, 'Ubley' from the Butcombe Junction Group, 'Blaenycwm' from North Gwent Railway Modellers and 'Cwmafon' from Mike Edge. 'Rassbottom Brow' from Arnold Bellfield and the Rassbottom Brow Group, 'Wetheral' from Newcastle and District M.R.S., 'Kenton' from Leamington and Warwick M.R.S. and 'Glenmore' from Peter Fletcher. The representative in 18.83 was the BR blue diesel period 'Lochend' from Ian Futers whilst our only 7mm layout was 'Southwold Light Railway' from John Dunford. New Traders included Nu-Cast, Specialised Products of Sheffield, Kean Maygib and a first appearance of the railway artist John Wigston. Static exhibits came from myself, Steff Torres and the Great Western Study Group.

Another feature of the Show Guide, that year, was a page article by myself entitled 'How do we begin', giving hints and tips of the bridge between the 'train set' and the 'layout' - I hope it was of use to someone!

We almost maintained our attendance figure that year and great hopes were being placed on our Silver Jubilee Show in 1987.

Why I was persuaded to move from Easter to late Spring Bank Holiday for this Show I cannot remember - it must have been that the M.R.C. were moving back to Easter and I felt honour-bound to move from their 'slot'. What I do know, is that the move was disastrous. Our attendance plummeted - from an already lowly 7809 of the year before - to 6041, the lowest we

1987

As well as my own 'Abbotsbury' were, 'Dentdale' by Dave Hackling, 'Gauxholme Viaduct' from Rochdale M.R.G., 'Hatfield Moor' from Alan Smith, 'Blaenycwm' from North Gwent, 'Chewton Mendip' from Bob Harper, 'Killaney' from Dave Walker, 'Monks Brewery' by Bob Dawson, 'Pine Creek' from Roger Nicholls, 'Petherick' from Barry Norman, 'Aspal' from Leamington and 'The Sidings' by Dave and Steve Peacey. 'Shadsworth Junction' came from Blackburn, 'Kirkham' from the Ebor Group and 'Traunsee' from Ian Futers. Silvermills (Otley) returned with static exhibits and Bruce Clarke's breakdown crane, and the Archbishop's Railway Circle did modelling demonstrations.

Dave Walker's 7mm Irish Broad Gauge Layout 'Killaney' in 1987.

have ever had since our first years in the Museum Rooms. It didn't help that we were more restricted than usual as two of the side areas in the Assembly Rooms, which we usually used as walkways, were not available because of structural repairs. It certainly wasn't that the exhibits were poor - fifteen layouts plus statics, demonstrations and full trade support.

I had been persuaded that, as it was the 25th Show, I should exhibit 'Abbotsbury'. I was also responsible for an article in the Show Guide '20 years on', which featured several photos connected to previous Shows. I organised competitions too, in conjunction with Radio York and they also provided an 'official Show opener' - one of the junior winners.

The most important ceremony, however, occurred on one of the mornings of the Show: One of our regular exhibitors, Dave Hackling, had been suffering from gout and had accidentally let slip that he was having to sleep with his foot in a cardboard box as it was far too painful otherwise. You can imagine his surprise when he arrived to be greeted by a large number of us, all with cardboard boxes on our feet, chorusing to a popular tune of the day; "Oh, we're living in a box...a cardboard box." He didn't forget that in a hurry!

Well, the situation with the lowest attendance ever, had to be faced up to. Firstly, good relations or not with the M.R.C., we *HAD* to return to the Easter slot. We did need help though, and it was to come from a different direction. Our friends from the Leeds Model Railway Society had gained support for their exhibitions from the Yorkshire Evening Post newspaper and I wondered whether there might be some 'mileage' in approaching them to assist us with publicity too. The outcome was that Yorkshire Post Newspapers became our first 'sponsors' and I shall be forever grateful to the Leeds lads for their understanding and support in this in allowing us to go down the same 'road' as themselves. It meant that, for 1988, we were able to expand back into two halls and over the usual four days. John and Owen Gibbon made a first appearance this year with a layout of their own 'Ruperra' in 0 gauge (although they had both been present for several years previously, with the Mid Gwent Group).

On the cover the Guide this year was Baz Ward's drawing of a father and son with a model train. This is one which has been used to good advantage on several occasions since and is one of my favourite drawings. Whilst on this topic I must mention Baz who, during this time, and for quite a number of years afterwards, was a staunch supporter of the Show and worked tirelessly for it - who can forget him; in cloak, top hat and all, treading the streets of York distributing handbills to everyone he met.

Baz Ward's fine drawing of a father and son looking at a model train.

He is one of the York Show's all-time real 'characters' and one whom, since his move to Greece, is sorely missed.

Another major change took place in 1988; for only the third time in the history of the Show we changed our Guide printers. I have already mentioned in previous chapters, our initial help from Joe Wilkinson, I have also talked of the assistance we received from Colin Judge of O.P.C. This was great, whilst O.P.C. had a stand at the Show - they could bring the guides with them - but it had proved a difficult task in subsequent years when I had to arrange collection from Headington. This I would do whilst attending exhibitions in reasonable proximity, or alternatively I would have to make a special journey to collect them. I am most grateful to Barry Oliver, who lived in Didcot during this period, for inviting me to stay with he and Hilary whilst on these forays. Thus, 1988 saw our move away from O.P.C. to Askews Printers of Doncaster. We have used this company up to the present time and they now produce all our publicity materials, signs etc. Under their guidance and with their support I have been able to create guides which have improved throughout the years and which have now become collectors items. I firmly believe we were the first to have a full colour Guide - in fact we may be the only Show to do this still. It can be costly but - if the product is good and worthy of the price - they will sell. Every year the guides have broken even on cost and always make a little extra.

1988

Twenty five layouts were included and the list is as follows; 'Steifelbahn' by Frank Wilkinson and A. Park, 'Buckden' by Nick Easton, 'Bredon' by A.C. Wood, 'Dovey Valley Railway', by Dick Wyatt and 'Benfieldside' by John H. Wright. In HO was 'Akten Vohwinkle' from the Western M.R.S., in N was Roger Nicholls' and Robin Nixon's 'Crystal Springs', 'Elton Moor' by the Elton Road Group from Bristol. 'Kirkham' by the Ebor Group returned for a second time. Layouts in EM included 'Dawarton' by Ray Ward and Bob Dawson, 'Fryupdale' by Paul Cope, 'Cromarty' by Rod Bellis and 'Chesil Town' by Mike Hayward. The Cardiff 4mm Group returned with 'Narberth' and John Brewer had 'South Devon 1885'. In 3mm was Peter Gentle's 'Mullion'. Jack Burnard and Maurice Bramley brought 'Houghton'. In the De Grey Rooms we had Ian Futers 'Saltskammergutbahn', Sandy Croall's 'Penlan', 'Macduff' from Leamington and Warwick M.R.S., Les Nehrlich, from Preston, with 'Llwyn Grug'. John and Owen Gibbon with 'Ruperra'. Demonstrations and displays by Barry Norman, Peter Kazer and my own display of the 25th anniversary of my 'South Devon Railway'. There were first time appearances for traders; Jackson Evans, Comet Coaches, Brian Badger, Modelex, A.F. Hammond, D & S Models, Cherry Scale Models, the North Eastern Railway Association and the Lancashire & Yorkshire Railway Society. Bill Hudson also mounted a display covering his recent Private Owner Wagon books.

Major winds of change were already beginning to blow during the 1989 Show. Rumour was rife that there was a distinct possibility the Assembly Rooms would be closed for a long period in order that the foundations could be strengthened. It seemed I might have to find an alternative venue - not an easy task. The Show, this year, included some 23 layouts together with demonstrations from myself on 'Sinnington - modelling the prototype' and the John and Gerry Show. Dave and Shirley Rowe exhibited 'Exebridge Quay' this year, but it was this layout that we had real difficulty getting into the Assembly Rooms. The Georgians (the Assembly Rooms date from

1989

Layouts included; 'Thorpe' from Leeds M.R.S., 'Hope Mill' from Martin Brent, 'Roe Pass' from Colin Hobson and 'Scotland Street' from Dave Elbourne. North Gwent R.M., had 'Leominster' whilst Roger Nicholls and Robin Nixon returned with 'Crystal Springs'. The Leamington club brought a 'Thomas the Tank Engine' layout complete with a real Fat Controller. Bill Evans of Elgee Hobbies had 'Obendorf' whilst Dick Wyatt returned for the 'umpteenth' time with 'Dovey Valley'. Chris Mansell brought 'Cannock Hawks Green' whilst Paul Cope returned with 'Fryupdale'. Gordon and Maggie Gravett with 'Llandydref', Normanton and Pontefract R.M.S. exhibited 'Ramsfield' whilst Dave and Steve Peacey returned with 'Highworth - Hannington'. In the De Grey Rooms you could have seen Radbroke Hall's 'Grinding Hault', Richard Deas' 'Littleborough', Ray Ward and Bob Dawson's 'Dawarton', Trevor Nunn's 'Wicken', Steve Barnfield's 'Colsterdale', Peter Thomas' 'Church Eaton', Bridgend M.R.C.'s 'Coaldale' and Keith Armes' 'Chipping Norton'. There were first trade appearances for Headstock Publications and Dart Castings.

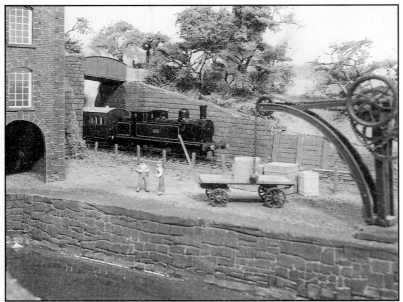

(Photo courtesy Railway Modeller)

'Church Eaton' by Peter Thomas, appeared at the 1989 Show.

that period) built doors a little narrower in width than doors usually are constructed today, and certainly much narrower than the baseboards Dave had constructed! What was more, Dave's boards could not be tipped sideways or vertically otherwise damage may occur. We did manage to get them through one way - the only layout where we had to use a shoe horn! Newcomers to the Show that year were my good friends Gordon and Maggie Gravett with 'Llandydref'.

After the end of the 1989 Show I recall that I had very mixed feelings. Firstly, mainly because of the involvement of Yorkshire Post Newspapers and the move back to two halls, we had turned the tide in attendance figures; a rise in 1988 of almost 4,000 had been followed by another increase of 800 in 1989. The only trouble was the worry over the venue for the 1990 Show. I must say here that, over the years we were in the city centre, I had great help and support from the Housing and Estates Department of the York City Council, especially Simon Williams. It was Simon who always ensured that the halls were available and gave me warnings of impending difficulties as early as possible. When a competitor attempted to 'cut the ground from under our feet' and book the halls immediately after the Show, Simon said we had already booked the halls. However, this was a 'little white lie', since we had not even had our committee meeting! He informed me of the repair work necessary to the buildings straight after the decision had been made. Thus it was that I had heard of the possible unavailability of the Assembly Rooms, though little did I realise, when we walked away from them in 1989, we would never again see a York Model Railway Show within their walls.

Soon after the close of the 1989 Show Simon was in touch; "What were we going to do?" he enquired, "What could we do?" I asked. His only suggestion was to take the Guildhall and the De Grey Rooms. This would definitely reduce the floor area available and could cause difficulties over unloading and loading, what was more, the Guildhall was 'hidden' behind the Mansion House, and not evident to prospective visitors. Beggars cannot be choosers, so we had to accept what we were offered; the De Grey Rooms (as usual), plus the Guildhall for the four days, and the Committee Rooms for three days (we could not use these on Tuesday as it was a working day). Exhibits had to be reduced in number, refreshment facilities had to be restricted - in fact, it was not a very happy outlook.

It was during the period before this Show that my mind ranged around all possible alternatives to the situation we were now in. I knew that if we

1990

In the Guildhall, that year, we featured 'Thomas the Tank Engine' from Leamington, 'Tipton Parva' from John and Jane Jacobs, 'Leominster' from North Gwent Railway Modellers and 'Windermere' from Nick Easton. David E. Jones' Lee Valley Crossing' featured along with Paul Jones' 'Hadley Town'. Gordon and Maggie Gravett returned with 'Llandydref'. The German Railway Society exhibited 'Alt Bayern' and Nick Hughes from the Normanton club 'Tilford Road'. Dennis Snook from Bristol had 'Calmsden' and John Watson showed 'Laxfield'. In the '3 days only' rooms were Paul Cope's 'Fryupdale', my own 'Sinnington' - modelling a prototype demonstration, and 'Goathland' from York Model Railway Society. In the De Grey Rooms we included the following; 'Bogsworth Junction' from Mike Sharman, 'Calverdale' from Andy Calvert, 'Newendon' in 2mm finescale from George and Barbara Nutter, 'Barnack' from Market Deeping M.R.C., 'Lochty Road' from Ian Futers, 'Grassington and Threshfield' by S.G. and D. Ross, 'Stanfield' by Robin Nixon, 'St. Nicklon' from Roger Nicholls and 'Racoon Valley RailRoad' from Mike Redsell. There was an addition to the trade as Cheltenham Model Railway Centre was included for the first time.

(Photo by Barry Norman courtesy Railway Modeller)

'Sinnington' was a departure from my love of the GWR. The prototype was close to my childhood home in North Yorkshire.

moved, as well as facing possible increases in costs, I would also face hostility from several of my committee of helpers who hated any change. I *DID* realise, though, that changes *WOULD* have to be made and, as usual, I had to be ready for their reservations and opposition. Thus it was that at the end of the 1990 Show Guide we announced that we would be moving to the York Racecourse for the 1991 Show. Unfortunately, because of all the difficulties, attendance again took a huge downward dip by nearly 3,000 folk.

I hope you will not mind if I end this chapter by quoting from the article 'Onward!' which featured on page 27 of the 1990 Show Guide;

"As many will already know through several articles which have been written over the past twenty eight years, the York Model Railway Show had its humble beginnings in the small Church Hall, in Front Street, Acomb in the early 1960s. After three years a move was made to the City Centre and the Museum Rooms (alas no more). Here it continued until 1972, the last two using the Museum Rooms and the Assembly Rooms. Closure of the Museum Rooms in 1972 meant that we had to continue in the Assembly Rooms only, and this we did spreading out into the De Grey Rooms in 1978, '79, '80. '81, '82, '83, '84, '88, and '89. We have not always been at Easter, though, despite many thinking that this is the case. We started as a Christmas period Show, moving after three years to February and only in 1969 did it move to the Easter Weekend period.

The Show has, over the years, become synonymous with both Easter and the Assembly Rooms which despite its 'palatial splendour' has had many drawbacks - not least being the many pillars which have caused much ribald comment from both exhibitors and visitors. Another 'feature' over the years has been the unevenness of the floor in the Assembly Rooms (especially in one area) coupled with the sagging of parts of the building and several cracks in the walls. We have noticed these over the years but it is only over the past few years that the Civic Authorities have set about tackling the reason and undertaking major structural work on the foundations. This originally was planned to take a year starting in April last but, as seems usual in these cases, the start was delayed and so it was that we learned in September that the Assembly Rooms would not be available to us in 1990. The Guildhall, though not completely suitable for our type of Show, was the only city centre venue which suited our needs at all. The Show's organisers do not anticipate using the Guildhall for more than the one year. There have been thoughts for some time about our future use of city centre venues. Although we are reluctant to loose the Assembly Rooms we do realise how difficult it is especially for the motorist. Car parking is difficult to find (and expensive) and it is also difficult to get about in the centre because of the queues. Over the past four years we have run a Visitor Survey which, amongst other things, has asked your feelings regarding the possibility of moving outside the city centre. We were very surprised to see how great a percentage felt it to be a good move. There is also a great deal of uncertainty regarding the availability of the Assembly Rooms after it reopens - whether it will become a permanent Exhibition/Museum or whether it will be let out to franchise. As we must know, at least a year before the Show, of our definite location, and bearing in mind many other factors, we have decided to move! Yes, the York Model Railway Show 1991 will be at the York Racecourse. It will be held in part of the Main Stand building and will have a far greater floor area than ever before. Coupled with this, there will be free parking for 800 cars and there will also be a special bus service which will bring visitors from the Railway Station and take any wives and families who do not wish to visit the Show into the city centre. There will also be full refreshment and bar facilities..."

It then goes on to say what exhibits had already been booked for the following year's Show. What had definitely not been stated to the visitors was the troubles which had been faced for years by exhibitors on both setting-up and packing-up days. At both the Assembly Rooms and De Grey Rooms there was no space whatsoever to park vans, cars, trailers and so forth. It was more than a little fraught and I can well remember, on setting-up day (Good Friday) that we always had to stop all action outside whilst the Good Friday Parade was made to the Minster. Moving in and out, we thought, would be a 'doddle' in future years - little did we know how we would have to improvise in those first years at the Racecourse - but that is for another chapter.

7

The Rough with the Smooth

I must admit that I approach this chapter with some hesitation, but I feel to leave it out would mean only a partial history of the Show. It's about the 'politics' behind the Show scenes, an aspect which many modellers prefer to stay well clear of, but something which has to be tackled in order to get decisions made and get things going. I would like to stress, though, that this is my memory and opinion of events, it may be that time will tell I was wrong - who am I to say? My only defence is that I did what I did at the time, not for personal gain, but for what I believed was the good of the Show and the hobby in general.

As I have already told; for the first few years of the Show I was sole organiser, provider, financier etc. Had there been a 'flop' I would have had to stand it financially from my own pocket, if I could of course. Therefore I soon began to seek relief from this situation. At the same time however, I was first in the field; it was through the first of the Shows that the York Model Railway Society, and later, the Ebor Group of Railway Modellers were formed. It was therefore difficult for them to promote their own exhibitions and this bore heavily on my conscience, especially as I was a member of both of the senior (as opposed to junior) groups for a time. After our move to the city centre I tried to involve the senior groups in the Show, but, apart from the Ebor Group, it was a fraught situation. The difficulty was that I ran the Shows only to further the good of the hobby, I had no other ulterior motive, such as making money for club funds, etc. When other adults became involved, their idea was basically to try and make as much as they could so that they could finance operations within their own club, therefore cutting their own expenditure on layouts, and so forth. The first involvement did not last long. I soon, though, became aware that I did need both their support and help - the Castle Railway Circle had only a small membership of juniors. Several dads did come along but we needed all the help we could get especially for setting-up, taking down and stewarding. It wasn't made easier by the fact that, for a great deal of the time, there were either two or three separate groups in the city and each had as much right of involvement as the other. Of the three groups the York Model Railway Society, after a short time, 'ploughed their own furrow' and organised their own exhibitions at another time of year. Several of their members have, from time to time, come along to

give us a hand and there was a time when they were in partnership but...
unfortunately, money matters always got the better of the relationship.

The York '0' Gauge Group had involvement in the 1980s (they were a
'breakaway' from the Ebor Group), several of them were on the organising
committee and did some good work for the Show. Once again, however,
money and lust for power began to prevail and, eventually, when I tried
(with the other committee members' support) to bring some sense to the
situation, we received their resignation and lost their valued assistance.
The final outcome was that we organised the Show with a completely
separate committee - The Friends of York Model Railway Show.

This committee included members from my own group, from the Ebor
Group and, at times, individuals from both the York Society and the York
'0' Gauge Group, but the groups themselves had no influence on our committee's thinking and actions.

At one time, if there was any excess of income over expenditure, it was
shared equally between the groups who had assisted with mounting the
Show but, recently, this excess has been used to establish a 'Rainy Day
Account', a fund which, recently, has seen us safely through one or two
very lean years, when we have either made a loss, or have just broken even
- as was the case at the beginning of the 1990s.

As is usual in many walks of life - if the 'status quo' is unsettled, there
are always those who seek change and this was certainly the case at the
end of the 1980s. Numbers were falling, profits were falling too and one
or two of the more recently affiliated members on the committee saw the
opportunity to force their influence on the situation. Thank goodness
however, I and a good number of long standing committee members, who
had been present for over a decade, realised what was happening. I think
this section quoted from my Show Manager's Report after the 1990 Show
gives an idea of what was happening;

"I was not, however, completely happy as I felt at all times under
scrutiny from one or two folk. Over the twenty seven years the Show
has been in existence I have completely enjoyed my part in organising
and running the Show. It has been the major achievement in my life
and one of which I am very proud. I am also pleased to have had
over the years several friends who have worked with me to make
the Show the great success it has been - I could not have done
everything without their support - they are the real Friends of the
York Model Railway Show.

The Rough with the Smooth

Latterly, though, I feel that a different mood is infiltrating into the happy atmosphere we have had for so many years. Ways in which things have been done most successfully for many years are being questioned and alternatives suggested when really they are not required. The reason that the York Show has been as successful as it has, and still is (I hope) is that a tried and tested organisation has been developed which is known to work.

It can be amended, if found necessary, but generally it is most successful. Now, it seems, there is an infiltration of 'change for change's sake' and if this course is continued, it could lead to the demise of the York Show as it is known and appreciated throughout the hobby.

I will do my best to ensure that this does not occur but I would like to feel that I had the rest of the committee behind me. I felt, throughout the Show, that my every action was being watched and notes made for future criticism. I was not the only person who noticed this and the action did little to enhance the usual relaxed and friendly atmosphere of the Show (I would like to add that the above was only by one or two folk and that happily all the rest of us worked together as we have normally done - thank heavens).

I would like to repeat that I will, for as long as I am able, continue to organise the York Model Railway Show to the best of my abilities, and to as great a standard as is possible, and hope that I will continue to have the support of all those who have given so much, for so long for the continued success of the Show."

It was during this period that I had moved away from running a model railway club for teenagers and juniors, and began modelling on my own. My situation had changed; I had taken early retirement from teaching and, although for the first few years, I still had lads whose interest continued, slowly for one reason or another, they left and were not replaced. I also moved from living with my sister and her husband to living on my own in the Malton area. The problem was that no longer having a club of my own, when the traumatic meeting occurred, I felt myself vulnerable. It was then that I began to receive messages of support and backing from the more longer established of our exhibitors. They didn't want to see the York Show change any more than I did. They enjoyed exhibiting at York, they enjoyed the social activities of the Easter weekend, and they were vehement in their support of myself and the Show.

The Show that Never Ends

Thus it was, at the 1990 Leamington Spa Exhibition, that the idea of the Friends of South Devon was conceived. It was to be a support group for myself and the York Show made up of members, not only from York but also from other parts of Great Britain, who would be available to assist with the Show and who would support me and my ideals. All of our regular exhibitors were contacted and, before long, a membership of some forty or fifty was established. This was just what was needed - I had a membership base to back me and could go into discussion not feeling a lone voice any more. It was good fortune that this did in fact occur as, before long, we began to realise that we really did need the support and help of these good folk. The York Show, today, would not be possible without their assistance.

The move to the Racecourse, brought everyone together again and, before long, those who sought to disrupt for their own advancement gave up and, for one reason or another, left the organisation. We faced the future better for this as, once again, everyone pulled together.

It was not until after the upheaval year of the electrical failure and the years that followed, that I was fully to understand how I was looked upon by my fellow committee members and I have to thank my good friend Owen for his observation and help with coming to terms with how best to approach those whom I, definitely, call my friends - but I have once again jumped in telling my story - so back once more to the early '90s.

8

The Past Decade

We moved to the Racecourse for the 1991 Show; not an easy move and one which was fraught with difficulties, especially ones concerned with the buildings themselves and with the fact that the 'old regime' - Messrs. Campbell and Arksey Senior - were still in charge there. Yes, we were the 'new boys on the block' and definitely under observation.

We were unable to use all of the facilities we would have liked and had to do with rooms and a situation which was far from ideal. The rooms we used that year were the '59 Bar and Ebor Bar, both were downstairs in the old stand which has now been demolished and replaced. From there, visitors had to venture back into the open air and climb an outside staircase to the Knavesmire Suite above the two bars. From there they traversed a short corridor before reaching the York and Ainsty Suite. Visitor refreshments and licensed bar were on other parts of the first floor. These were now out of our control; one of the drawbacks of moving to the Racecourse was that we could no longer provide our own refreshments for visitors, the franchisees at the Racecourse, York Banqueting, have the sole right to do this. We were however allowed to supply liquid refreshments, free, to our exhibitors and stewards, and this we did - but only this. The main area, downstairs underneath the York and Ainsty Suite, was unavailable to us during the first two years and I remember, definitely, that there were other functions on at the same time as ours. They also used most of the yard area and caused several problems for us. Fortunately, the 'Outdoor Exhibition' (in more ways than one) did not do very well and did not return in 1993 allowing us to have the large ground floor area ourselves - but I am jumping ahead again...

As we did not have the outside area immediately in front of the halls we were using, we had to have something to attract folk to our end of the complex. I hit on the idea of inviting a fairground organ - that would give plenty of noise and attract the few casual visitors that were around! Me being me, I had to go for the best, and managed to interest the Show Organ Society who brought White Bros. Mammoth Gavioli along. I also invited the Whitwell's Clayton Shuttleworth 'Wold Ranger' road locomotive to partner the organ, but I regret it was not up to generating enough electricity to keep the organ running, and they had to recourse to their own generators. The local branch of the North Yorkshire Moors R.P.S. owned, at that time, a vintage road coach which they took to outdoor events as a sales coach to

Hull Miniature Railway Society's 7mm Irish Narrow Gauge layout 'Kerry Bridge' was one of the layouts at the first York Show at the Racecourse.

raise funds for the railway; we included that, together with the Passenger Carrying Track of the Leeds and District S.M.E.E.

This Show was one of the very few which had an official opening. The truth was, we felt that we ought to let as many folk as possible know that we had moved and I therefore invited David Dunning of B.B.C. Radio York to come along and do the honours. It must have done the trick, for our attendance rose by almost 1000. Of course we were still enjoying the support of Yorkshire Post Newspapers and this would also have had something to do with the increase. Once again we ran for the three and a half days, as we had done in the city centre. The list of exhibits on the Show 'bill' is extensive and really does command the whole panel to itself.

The following year, 1992, despite the continued involvement of the Yorkshire Post Newspapers, attendance was 1500 down on the year before. This was despite the inclusion of what we thought were some of the very best layouts from across the country. I have tried hard to find a reason for the drop, but I can recall nothing of great importance. There is a note, though, in the 'attendance book' which states "Recession" so that could have been it!

1991

In the Ebor Bar and '59 Bar I included, 'Bad Heiligenstadt' from Doctor Mike Watts, Barrie Kelsall's 'Filisur', 'Bishport' from Taunton M.R.G., 'Skipdale' from Bob Dawson and the well-known 'Kerry Bridge' from Hull Miniature Railway Society. Trade in this area included; Yorkshire Post Newspapers, Formil M.E., Brian's Kits & Bits, Milnsbridge Models, Geo. Norton, C & G Models, the Ebor Group secondhand stand and the Cheltenham Model Centre.

Going up the stairs we found, in the Knavesmire Suite; 'Kenton' from John Watson, 1950s Hornby Dublo from North Gwent, 'Wiswell Bridge' from Normanton and 'Cardigan' from the Cardiff 4mm Group. Barry Norman did a modelling demonstration and three other layouts were exhibited; Dave Elbourne's 'Scotland Street', 'Dunnan Lane' from Chris Dunne and Derek Lane and Dave & Steve Peacey's 'G.C.S. Quarry'. Trade here, came from Ratio, Dart Castings and Shire Scenes, R.S.B. Models and Parkington Books.

Along the corridor, in the York and Ainsty Suite, were traders; C & L Finescale, Jackson Evans, Headstock Publications, GEM Model Railways, Railway Modeller, World of Miniatures, R.C.T.S., Video 125 and Proops. Layouts included Arthur Barrow's 'West Jayton', 'Nearly Whitby' from Paul Cope, 'Littleborough' from Richard and Christine Deas, John Brewer and Tony Rowles brought 'Het Spoor' and Gordon and Maggie Gravett with the first appearance of 'Half Term at Ditchling Green'. Also featured in this area were Trevor Hughes' 'Tan Y Grisiau', 'Combe Mellin' from the Ipsley Circle, 'Tolgooth Road' from Kevin Price, 'Shallowford Park' from Walter Pullman (this was featured in full colour on the Guide cover). 3mm was represented by 'Avon Street' from the Bristol area, whilst John and Stella New had their Hornby Dublo 'Classic Train Set'. To complete, there were static exhibits and modelling demonstrations by Leeds M.R.S. members, the Gauge 0 Guild display and railway art from Mr Wigston, trade from Modelex, Wakefield Model Railway Centre, Photo-Rail Processing and Slaters Plasticard plus two more layouts; 'Tenter Brow' from the Rassbottom Brow group and 'Piel Quay' from Bill Pierce.

Once again we had the Gavioli to attract folk to our section of the grounds. This year it was 'partnered' by black Fowler Showman's engine 'Repulse' and very fine they looked together. The Leeds S.M.E.E. passenger-carrying track also featured although they found it a little chilly at times!

There were several changes in the trade stands attending in '92. Out went Cheltenham Model Centre, World of Miniatures, Proops and Photo-Rail Processing and in came N Gauge Lines, The Signalman, Colin Ashby, Eileen's Emporium and D & S Models - most of whom have been regulars since that year. Despite the drop in attendance 1992 was, I feel, a special year. Not counting the EMGS, Gauge '0' Guild, Modelling Demo's from

1992

The John and Gerry Show, Ray Ward and Bob Dawson's 'Hallfield Road', Dr. Michael Watts' 'Charmes', Pete McParlin's 'Snake River', 'Ronsthorpe' by Ron Bailes, Keith Gowen's 'Helston', 'Hardwick' from Normanton and Ray and Cida Earl's 'Penny Hassett' - these were downstairs. Upstairs were; 'York North and West' from Gary Hall, John Bowden's 'Langton Herring', 'G.C.S. Quarries' from the Peaceys, 'Swn Y Mor' from North Gwent, 'Abergynolwyn' from the Gravetts, 'Het Spoor' from John Brewer and Tony Rowles, 'Lydham Heath' from Barry Norman and 'Sinnington' from yours truly - I believe the last time one of my own layouts has featured at a York Show as a working exhibit. Peter Kazer's 'Corris', Shirley Rowe's 'Catalunya', 'Nailsworth' from the Gloucester/Avon 3mm Group, 'Leeds Trams' from Andy Ross, 'Brushford' from Andy Cooper, 'Benfieldside' from John H. Wright and 'Copenhagen Fields' from the Model Railway Club completed the working models.

(Photo courtesy Railway Modeller)

Peter Kazer's authentic model of Corris took over ten years to build.

members of the Hull M.R.S. and the N.E.R.A. stand, twenty four stands were featured. Read the listing in the panel and I'm sure that you'll agree with me that it was a first class Show; no wonder, in my Show Manager's report, commenting on the low attendance, I said that it was the public's loss, not ours.

1993 and we were still attempting to establish ourselves away from the city centre. This year we had cut our ties with the Yorkshire Post; it just wasn't sensible for either of us to continue the arrangement - neither received any benefit. Instead we had arranged for the Yorkshire Evening Press Bus to appear in the yard along with the Gavioli, 'Repulse' and all the usual outside attractions. This year, the major change was that there were no counter-attractions within the complex and we had use, for the first time, of the oddly-shaped ground floor area of the '59 Stand. We gave up the use of the '59 Bar and the Ebor Bar, but continued to use the areas we had done in the first two years at the Racecourse on the first

1993

Layouts downstairs included; 'Ashford in the Water', Clay Cross M.R.S., 'Newandold', Warley M.R.C., 'London Road', 'Leighford', Wolverhampton M.R.S., 'Wheal Louise' by Robert Tivendale, 'Bonchester Bridge' by Brian Sunman, 'Annswick' by Colin Stark, 'Marston Abbots' by Bob Beaumont and John Shelley, 'Alresford' by Basingstoke and N. Hants M.R.S., 'Avyn a Llyin' by David Bailey, the 'Gilling Railway' by Paul Cope, 'Kirkham' by The Ebor Group, 'Wellington' by David Amias and 'Midsomer Norton' by the Portsmouth and South Hants Rly. Circle. Upstairs could be found; 'Spoorlin Haven' by John Brewer and Tony Rowles, 'Penford' by Brian Moss, 'Neumakt' by Ian Futers, 'Barrowfleet', 'Madestone Road' from L. and D. Darbyshire, 'Cwm Fyddl' from Ron Oliver, 'Lower Loxley' by Ray and Cida Earl, 'Half Term at Ditchling Green' by Gordon and Maggie Gravett, 'Tregoran' by Alan Searle, 'Ynysybwl Fach' by Owen and John Gibbon, 'The Sidings' by Dave and Steve Peacey, 'Swyn Y Mor' returned from North Gwent, 'Ilam' from John Degg and Bill Wood, 'Umbridge' that curiously crazy layout in 16mm Narrow Gauge from Peter Butler, 'Maristowe and Coldrennick Road' from Bob Harper, 'Tetley Town' from Bob Dawson, 'Great Marston', A. Bailey and lastly, 'Karlsberg' from Normanton and Pontefract R.M.S. Non layout stands also appearing were N.E.R.A., E.M.G.S., Duel and Isotrain Demonstration and demo's by Dave Lowery, the H.M.R.S., and the 3mm Society.

floor, i.e. the York and Ainsty Suite and the Knavesmire Suite. New in the trade this year, were Cove Models, London Road Models, A1 Models, Woodhead Models, Sharman Wheels (under new management), Westdale & Haye Developments, Oakville/PMK/Connoisseur Models and Squires Model & Craft Tools, and we lost The Signalman. Attendance was very slightly up - by 32 folk only - a great pity, for those who didn't come missed another very high standard Show.

We made a loss in 1994; attendance was down by 300 and we had not increased entrance charges, as perhaps we should have done. Luckily our high interest (Rainy Day) account saved us from going under. I have Joe Wills to thank for his keenness to create this account. I notice also that, this year, Fiona Ellis and Jeanette Wood had taken the job of security.

Mr Campbell was still in charge at the Racecourse but a new name, N. Johnson, had replaced J. Arksey who had retired. We had been informed, before this Show, that we would be losing some of our usual areas in the following year. This was because of the demolition and reconstruction work which would lead, eventually, to a completely new Knavesmire stand.

1994

The trade representation was much as in the past years but with Modelling Railways Illustrated, Oakwood Press and Videos, Martin Finney, 4D Ltd., Crownline, Woodhead Models, British Railway Modelling, D & E Videos, Crest Models, Alan Gibson and Squires Models and Craft Tools ringing the changes. Societies included; The Gauge '0' Guild (York Area)., N.E.R.A., R.C.T.S., E.M.G.S., 3mm Society, H.M.R.S. and the 2mm Finescale Association. Static exhibits and demonstrations came from Wolverhampton M.R.C., York and District S.M.E.E., The Ebor Group of Railway Modellers and Bob Dawson.

Layouts included; 'Hardwick', 'Wedmore', 'Hadley Town', 'Horndon', 'Morris Illinois', 'Linfit West', 'Leeds Trams', 'Deepcar', 'Wetherby', 'Sidney Park', 'Chelthwaite and Beccadale', 'Blaenycwm', 'Boosedale' and 'Botzingen am Kaiserstuhl' on the Ground Floor. 'Akten Vohwinkel', 'Credibility Gap', 'Strone Ferry', 'Striving', 'Port Victoria, 'Hudson Lane', 'Kirkhamgate', 'Glenmore', 'Nearly Whitby', 'Rushenden Metals', 'Newcastle Haymarket', 'Nether Stowey', 'Merlin Park' and 'Rhosteigne'. 'Helston', 'Everingham' and 'Church Fenton' were scheduled for the Knavesmire Suite but the former had to be withdrawn because of Keith Gowen's ill health.

Such upheaval had become usual with our Show - we never had a long period in which to settle down. I believe that, until recently, we have never had more than two or three consecutive years without disruption of one sort or another; York Model Railway Show really has survived against all the odds.

Once again, we featured the Mammoth Gavioli Organ but, because of trouble with water and oil spilt onto the tarmac the previous year, we did not invite a showman's engine to power the organ. The passenger carrying line again ran close to the Show.

The following year we did, in fact, lose a good part of the York and Ainsty Suite and the whole of the Knavesmire Suite. The Racecourse authorities did go out of their way to assist us find replacement areas and the Show 'went up in the world'- as high as the fourth floor of the main stand and the Shirley Heights Suite!

The Show Guide in 1995 was the first to include colour pictures within its pages. For the first time I included the plans for the different areas on the centre spread of the Guide - this suggestion had come, originally, from Dick Dring and proved to be an extremely good move - so much so that it has been the norm ever since. This year saw Show Guide sales being done by members of my Junior Longsword Team - and a good job they made of it too. Outdoors we had the usual attractions - the Gavioli and the passenger-carrying line from Leeds and District S.M.E.E.

This was the year of... the flyposting incident. The authorities at the Racecourse have been very tolerant of much that we have done. They do not like, however, to have posters plastered on the walls of the rooms, especially those where new, expensive, wallpaper has been hung! It was towards the end of the Show that it was discovered that posters advertising both the Wales and West of England Exhibition and also the Keighley M.R.S.'s next event had been placed on the walls and pillars using a strange type of Blu-tack. It wouldn't have been so bad if normal Blu-tack had been used as this is removable, with great care. The stuff that was used was purple in colour and left horrible marks however careful you were with it. Needless to say the Racecourse authorities found out and were not amused; I was instructed to furnish them with contact addresses and I know that real problems ensued - fortunately our good relations with the Racecourse authorities remained intact - but I still wonder if the outcome might have been different. That is why I am now always so insistent that posters etc., be handed in to us so that we can put them up ourselves in places where we have pre-arranged with the authorities. Even so there are

1995

Layouts on the ground floor that year included 'Maristow and Coldrennick Road', 'Runswick Bay', 'Corcadoragha', 'Lynton and Lynmouth', 'Sonley', 'Cwm Fyddl', 'Wistow', 'Dewsbury', 'Cherry Orchard', 'Kimmeridge', 'Ynysybwl Fach' together with static exhibits from York and District S.M.E.E. and demonstrations from Derek Mundy, Steve Barnfield, Gordon and Maggie Gravett and the Gauge 0 Guild. The Railway Modeller and British Railway Modelling stands were also down here together!

In an expanded York and Ainsty Suite we featured 'Hollybank Depot', 'Llwynmawr', 'Lakey Hill', 'Sundown', 'Aberdare', 'Devils Creek', 'Reighton', 'Adavoyle Junction', 'Penelau Fach', Chris Lammacraft's 'Ashburton' and 'Hartwell'. There were also static exhibits and the E.M. Gauge Society demonstrations.

The second floor and third floor had very little on them, for we could only use the stairwell areas. The Shirley Heights Suite on the fourth floor, however, had the following layouts; 'Salehurst', 'Wanborough Camp', 'Dyke Road', 'Yatbury', 'Minsterley', 'Alnhill', 'Hawes' and 'Inkaston Moor'. Also featured were Mr Wigston the artist, the N Gauge Society and the H.M.R.S., plus several trade stands.

(Photo courtesy Continental Modeller)

Roger Nicholls' American H0 layout 'Sundown' appeared this year.

still one or two unthinking folk who each year put posters either in the wrong places or with the wrong materials - will folk ever learn about flyposting?

We had to raise the prices in 1995, following our losses of 1994. Part of my introduction in the Show Guide reads as follows;

"I must also pass on the organisers' regrets that we have had to raise (admission) prices this year. This has been forced upon us by our making quite a sizeable loss in 1994. The cost of mounting the Show runs into many thousands of pounds and, contrary to belief in some quarters, no individual makes money on the venture - in fact the fourteen organising 'Friends' put in a great deal of effort throughout the year to bring you the very best Show possible. This they do with no financial or other gain apart from sharing with you the great enjoyment of being part of an excellent display of all that is best in the Model Railway Hobby - long may it continue."

Most of the trade support remained the same each year but, in 1995, we had one or two changes. Out went Brian's Kits and Bits, Oakwood Press, Martin Finney, 4D Ltd. and Sharman Wheels. In came Green Scene, Railwayania, Langley Miniature Models, S & D Models, Timbercraft, Andy Duncan and Model Signal Engineering.

Being on numerous floors was not as difficult as it might have been. Between some of the floors there were escalators and there were also lifts to all floors plus, of course, normal stairs.

Numbers of visitors stayed almost constant that year - we only had an increase of about 30 across the four days we were open.

I feel that it is appropriate here to mention the great loss we sustained between the 33rd and 34th Show. For many years I had relied upon the assistance of several members of the Friends of York Model Railway Show to put the Show together, run the Show, and take it apart when it finally closed. Amongst the keenest of these people was Bernard Richmond, a fine modeller and a keen supporter of the Show who had been involved since the 1960s. It was in the summer immediately after the 1995 Show that we were all very surprised and upset to hear of Bernard's illness - something he'd contracted as a consequence of working with asbestos during his years when he tended the heating boilers at Bootham Hospital. Bernard suffered much over the following months, but such was his keenness, that through to the end he would demand that the minutes and agendas of meetings should be sent to him. He bore his great suffering well and, when he eventually passed away in the autumn of the year we decided that we should award an annual plaque to the layout in the Show which he would have found the most interesting - and this continues to this day.

A great deal has altered since Bernard was around - we no longer construct our 'man-size Meccano' barriers for a start. The Show has grown too since Bernard's death - I wonder what he would think of it now? I am sure he would still admonish me in his inimitable way for using my 'elastic tape measure' when planning the Show.

Yes, Bernard, we still miss you.

9

Who Turned the Lights Off?

1996 was the year we approached with great apprehension. Already I knew we would have to build high - in fact it had been necessary to plan the Show on five floors. What was more, we had great difficulties getting the exhibits into the different areas because of extensive restrictions in the outdoor areas - the usual yard was 'out of bounds' as it was a building site. Everyone had to come through the gateway close to the triangle at the junction of Knavesmire Road and Campleshon Road. Vans and lorries had to be programmed so that an even flow could be achieved; I am very grateful to my friend, John Gibbon, who has a great deal of experience in these circumstances and he, together with myself, organised things so that there were very few hitches on either setting-up day, or on the Tuesday after everyone had packed up. In fact, it might be said that this was one of the better outcomes from this year, for, having become conscious of the situation we have continued to regulate deliveries and collections every year since, thus making for an easier and smoother flow of traffic.

Things worked quite well on the Thursday and Friday, despite the limitations placed upon us by the rebuilding programme (for this not only included the new stand being built, but also parts of the stand which we were using). We went to our accommodation on the Friday evening feeling quietly confident that things were going to go O.K., but little did we know...

Saturday came and the Show opened, as usual, at 10.00 am. There was a good number of visitors, as was always the case on the Saturday (which has been our busiest day for quite a number of years). Having seen the start-up work well, and there being no queries, problems or such, I decided to make my official 'round' of the exhibits to wish everyone "Good Morning," and ask if everything was O.K. My office was in one of the private boxes on the second floor level. I decided to start on the fifth floor and work downwards to the ground floor.

As was usual, I took the lift. Everything seemed to be O.K. There were few problems, if any. Right, the first floor was next; I would do the intermediate landings later. Four young children were waiting for the lift on the fifth floor, two girls and two boys. I asked them if I could join them in the lift; perhaps they would volunteer their feelings about the standard of the Show - I always sought opinions from the visitors, especially children as I found them to be the most frank and honest. We passed the intermediate floors and had almost reached the first floor when the lift ground to a halt; it had stopped between floors. Luckily, I had my two-way radio with me and was able to call up others on the organising team. They reported that the whole of the electrics had cut out on all but the top floor. I was stuck and had to depend on others to get things sorted - something my team were not used to doing as generally, they sought my approval before taking action. It was finally decided to contact the Fire Service to get us out of the lift and, having contacted the Racecourse representative he then volunteered the information that the site electrician would have to be called out - and he was in Halifax!

Luckily there was an emergency light in the lift but it was interesting to see the different reactions of the children to the situation. One of the boys was very tearful whilst the other remained cheerful throughout the hour we spent entombed and tried his hardest to keep the others cheerful too. The girls were very quiet and I knew, from my teaching experience, that too much questioning would soon bring the tears flowing.

Whilst I was in the lift I was kept informed of what was happening. It seems the ground floor was the worst hit, as there were no windows there and thus was very little daylight. The top floor, though, continued to work reasonably normally, and it also had the most windows, folk were still happy there. The first floor was gloomy, where windows were few. The reactions of the visitors were mixed. Some accused ourselves of the fault, some demanded the return of their admission fee but most were happy to go along with the situation until it was resolved.

The Fire Service eventually arrived - not before time, as it happened, as a few minutes before the temporary lighting in the lift had failed and one, at least, of the girls was in near hysterics. It took the combined efforts of one of the boys and myself to keep an even keel - telling jokes and funny stories to keep the others amused. The firemen managed to open the door; we were only a few feet away from the first floor and were soon out. Then it was that I had to try and sort things out - and I was not in the best shape to do so.

Luckily Owen Gibbon came to the rescue and he, along with other members of the committee and the Friends, managed to sort things out. The duty electrician duly arrived from Halifax and we were back in business. The only thing was we had lost about two hours of time and had not given a good impression to our visitors; and it wasn't our fault either!

The cause of the major blow-out came to light later: It seems that, because of the building of the new Knavesmire Stand, it had been necessary to put our stand on a temporary electrical feed. This had been adequate until the caterers had switched on all their heated cabinets at about 11.00

am. The demand for power was too great and resulted in the main fuses blowing. Carlo, of York Banqueting, would have none of this, though; it was not their fault, he stated! It was, however, proved to be the case later in the day, for, when the cabinets were switched on again for a Wedding Reception in the Gimcrack Rooms; the electricity again failed. Once again we had to wait whilst the electrician came from West Yorkshire! What's more, after he had repaired the fuse, and whilst he was on his way out of York, another breakdown occurred and he had to be called on his mobile phone. On his return, he was then instructed by his superiors that he was *NOT* to leave the building until the Show closed for the day, and that he was to be in attendance for the rest of the weekend. By then the damage had been done; although that weekend we had increased our attendance figures by over 1,000, because of the calamity, attendance figures dropped again next year.

The happenings of '96 did have some good implications. We became more conscious, for the years following, of the importance of our safety policy and of our arrangements in case of fire. We have learned how much we need the help of certain folk and I, definitely, have learned my own limitations! It has also made us a great deal more conscious of policies concerning car parking, moving in and packing up, and of general stewarding.

Throughout the rest of the weekend we were 'on tenterhooks' waiting for something to happen, but it didn't. What few of us knew, at the time, was that the electricians had been in overnight on the Saturday and had strengthened the electricity supply. We took no chances though, we tried to save on electricity wherever possible. We used one lift only, and Owen Gibbon, John Hughes and Gethin Williams took it in turn to be the 'bell boys' operating the lift manually, thus saving electricity. As I wrote in my introduction to the Show Guide in 1997; you wouldn't have realised, on any of the other three days, there had been such trauma on the Saturday. But, as I stated above, the damage had been done and we were further back, attendance wise, than we had been the year before.

It was a good Show in 1996 too. None of our traders left us that year and we were joined by Parkside Dundas and Wild Swan Publications. Eight pages of the Guide had full colour pictures. Bernard Richmond and John Robinson were both remembered (both had been stalwart supporters of the Show and both had passed away during the previous winter months) and Fiona, for the first time in a long time, was not in the List of Officials. Outdoors we had the Gavioli but no passenger carrying line.

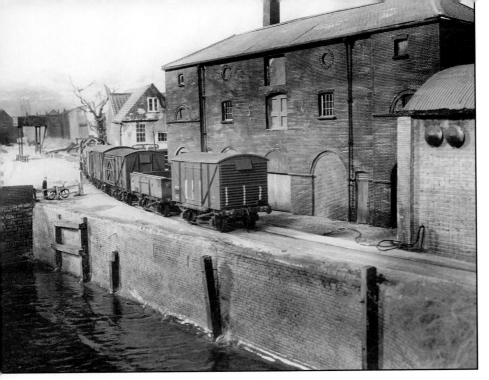

John Shaw, the present Show Treasurer and supporter from the early days, brought his wonderfully atmospheric 4mm layout 'Albion Street' in 1996. Here, published for the first time, are some views of the layout which features several prototype buildings from around the York area.

During the run of the Show, I was invited by Nick Johnson to go with him and have a look at the new stand which he felt would suit our needs much better than the one we were currently using. I was horrified to see the number of pillars involved in the building - shades of the Assembly Rooms, I felt. But Nick allayed my fears, saying it would be much better when finished.

In retrospect, I now realise that 1996 proved that I was not infallible. The Show was growing and I was ageing. I would need to take more care in future years and learn to depend more on others to do the jobs which were becoming more difficult for me to do. I also believe that the committee members from York began to realise that they needed greater help and support from those from further afield to assist with the running of the Show. It had grown and in the new stand it could grow even more. We were going to need all the help we could get and, if it meant having to depend more on those from away - then so it would be.

Another problem area was the construction of the Handiangle barriers. This, because of the growing size of the Show, was becoming more and

1996

Amongst the layouts on the ground floor were 'Newcastle N.B.' from Ian Futers, 'College Grove' from Allan Redgwick, 'Chee Tor' from Manchester M.R.S., 'St. Mellion' from Richard and Sue Andrews and 'Sonley' from S. and D. Models. Skipton club showed 'Lofthouse in Nidderdale', John Smith, 'North Foreland', Barry Norman, 'Lydham Heath', Steve Sims, 'Bleadon', Warley M.R.S., 'The Flat Tor & Otterspool Railway' and the Invicta Group, '70J Elms Lane M.P.D.' Mike Williams brought his 'Minima Bay'. On the First Floor were 'Cadeleigh' by Barry Foster, John Shaw's 'Albion Street', 'Jamaica Reach' from the North Devon M.R.S., 'Lesser Wenlock' by David Stone, 'Meon' from South Hants M.R.S., 'Coedway' from Phillip George, 'Inver' by John Seward, Andy Ross' 'Leeds Trams' in extended form, North Gwent's 'Penelau Fach', 'Trehayne' from Bodmin and District M.R.C., 'Calne' from Chris Hewitt and 'Middlepeak' from Geraint Hughes. There were no lay-outs on the second, third or fourth floors but, on the fifth floor could be found 'Midford' by the North Cheshire Group, 'Hochdorf' by Peter Kirby, 'West Park' from Hull M.R.S., 'Grove Park' from Weston Railway Modellers, 'Zillis Rhb' from Phil Donvaband and 'Tywyn Wharf to Pendre' from the Talyllyn R.P.S.

more of a demanding task. John Lundie and Andy Crawshaw had found it very difficult that year and we were all concluding that an alternative would have to be found.

Thank goodness for our friendship with Warley M.R.C., this has meant that, since that time, we have been able to hire their barriers for a very reasonable fee and to use them instead of the unwieldy Dexion. It is said, that good comes out of bad, and thus it was in our case. We learned much from that calamitous year all of which put us in good stead for the future.

10

After the Storm

The 'happenings' of 1996 have influenced the running of the Show ever since; of that, there is no doubt. For a start I began, slowly, to really value the assistance of others. The only trouble was that I had had so many disappointments in the past that I was loathe to trust anyone to do anything. This was all very well in the preparatory work and still is (in fact, I prefer it that way), but, when it came to the actual setting up and running of the Show I knew I couldn't manage things without help.

Over the next five years I learned to increasingly trust others more, I realised too, just how much they stood behind me and appreciated what I did. My style of management began to change and I was able to depend on folk more to carry out the tasks in the Show they had offered to undertake. My confidence in others grew so that when we eventually reached the Show in 2001 I was able, happily, to leave the actual running of the Show very much in their hands. I was there as 'ultimate' to make final decisions as Show Manager, but the smaller decisions I could happily leave to them; they knew what to do. This, as I say, has not been easy, but I am most grateful to all those who give so much of their time, share the same values and aims as myself for the Show. They work tirelessly in the day before the Show, during the Show, and after its close, making the event successful and entertaining for the visiting public and ensuring a smooth operation for our exhibitors and traders. But, as has been usual in this story, I have again jumped ahead again; so back to 1997...

The attendance, that year, was down 450 - I must say I had expected it to be more! There had been change at the Racecourse in that Mr. Campbell had retired and been replaced by Phillip Smedley who seemed far more supportive of our efforts - Nick Johnson continued as our main contact.

This year saw our first, tentative, moves into the new Knavesmire Stand. We only used part of the ground floor here - York Banqueting used the main part for visitors catering. We also used the first floor mezzanine level for exhibits but retained the ground floor and the York and Ainsty Suite in the old stand we had previously used. Once again the Gavioli played outside, but there was again no passenger carrying line. If I may quote here from the introduction page of the Show Guide of that year:

"Over the years, both in the city centre and in our present venue, we have had to suffer restrictions, alterations, or loss of space at the

1997

Layouts were as follows; on the ground floor of the New Knavesmire Stand, 'Ruyton Road' by J. Spencer, 'Inverbucket' by B. Ellingworth, Warley M.R.C.'s 'Temple Dean', 'Askrigg Bank' from Kendal M.R.C., T Couling's 'Port St. George', 'Monkswood Mill' from John and Jane Jacobs, 'Brookfield' from Ray and Cida Earl, Bill Rankin's 'Baldown Junction, 'Franklinsberg' from J.H.Wright, 'Welham Green T.M.D.' from M. and A. Calvert, Steve Flint's 'Reighton', 'Yeominster' from D. Richards, Keith Gowen's 'Helston', 'Karlsberg' from Normanton and Pontefract R.M.S., 'Lynford Junction' from S. Wright and Ian Morris' 'Morris Illinois'.

On the mezzanine level were to be found trade stands and the stands of other societies and preserved railways. In the York and Ainsty Suite were Dave Sutton's 'Sonley', D. Taylor's 'Charmouth', Paul Jones' 'Hadley Road', 'Mellin Quay' by the Ipsley Circle, 'Penrhiwceiber Twlch' from John and Owen Gibbon, 'Yaxbury Branch' from Jas Millham, 'Gas Works' from Yeovil M.R.G., Trevor Hughes with 'Tan Y Grisiau', 'Nether Scratching' by Lol Soccamondo and Gordon and Maggie Gravett with 'Half Term at Ditchling Green', plus numerous demonstrations in this area.

On the ground floor of the old stand were; 'Sidney Park' from Roger Ellis, the Ebor Group's 'Whitfford', 'Alton' from the Railway Enthusiasts Club, 'Aberdare' from Cardiff 4mm Group, 'Skenfrith' from North Gwent R.M., 'Market Lindum' from our friends in Hull M.R.S., 'Ballyfoyle' from I. Hallworth, 'North Holderness' from Don Annison and Phil Steen, 'Danby Dale' from F. Auffret and D. Johnson and Brian and Phillip Parker's 'Melbridge Dock'.

very last minute; never since 1971 when we lost the Museum Rooms have we really had a Show as I would have liked it. But now, for the first time in 26 years, I look forward to a Show as I feel it ought to be presented (I write this quite some time before the Show and sincerely hope I do not live to regret these words!!!)."

I didn't, although we did have several layout withdrawals that year and the trade had one or two changes, too. We lost Woodhead Models and our good friend Roy Dock of G.E.M. who had to retire. British Railway Modelling joined us as did Phoenix Precision Paints, Chowbent Castings, Comet Models and Model Railway Enthusiast; the latter stand was run by folk who were more used to swapmeets and who decided to pack up early

on the Tuesday as they were doing little trade! We also had our usual support from the preservation movement, scale societies and so forth plus, of course, our usual displays of static models.

Our very first 'All Colour' Show Guide appeared in 1998; this heralded our complete move into the new Knavesmire Stand our 'home' since that time. Attendance was up slightly, that year, by 176. This Show saw a change in chief door steward. Shortly after the 1997 Show Gordon Gomersall our chief door steward since 1995, when he had taken over from Ray and Judith Wardell (who themselves had been our door stewards since the early days), said he wished to call it a day. Gordon was also the person who had been in charge of ticket sales organisation and our auditor since the late 1980s. He had been a great friend of Bernard Richmond and, I felt, had not been completely happy since Bernard's tragic death. He had been a good worker for the Show, and a great supporter, and I was loathe to see him go as were the rest of the 'Friends'. We were very lucky when Rupert Brown offered to take his place. Although Rupert came from York originally, he was now working in London and proved, once again, that you need not be a York resident to be an active participant in the running of the Show, especially with all the modern communications technology now available.

This year we used, much to the chagrin of York Banqueting, the whole of the ground floor. Visitors refreshments went to the third floor restaurant area where they have stayed since that time. This year we began to 'claw back' the number of visitors but only by 176. The cost of hiring the facilities had also risen - by over a third and so we had to make a hefty (for us) increase on admission fees. 1998 also saw the emergence of our 'Supporters'. For more years than I care to mention, we had had the support of the Railway Modeller and Peco but, in our move to a new stand, we felt we needed further support. This was forthcoming initially from Railwayania and Squires Model & Craft Tools then, in 1998 from Bachmann Industries Europe. We are very grateful to all our 'Supporters' for the assistance they have given us over the past few years. This has enabled us to do things, both materially and publicity-wise which we would not, otherwise, have been able to do. Since that time the Bachmann Display Stand has been a feature of our ground floor area showing everything available from this forward-looking firm.

'Reighton', by Steve Flint, is an EM gauge layout portraying the British Rail era in the early 1980s. It made its second appearance at the York Show in 1997.

We used the whole of the ground floor, that year, plus the first floor mezzanine level, the first floor itself and the second floor mezzanine level. We had 38 layouts on display and 104 stands altogether. Outdoors the Gavioli still continued its tunes being joined by Stephan Torres' York Pullman coach. Trade continued in 1998 much as in past years but with

1998

On the ground floor; 'Kellerton on Sea' from North Devon M.R.C., 'Happisburgh' from the Model Railway Club, 'Hinton St. Mary' by R. Pearson and G. Reed, 'Stoke Summit' from Wolverhampton, 'Halesowen' from Warley, Trevor Nunn's 'East Lynn', 'Cedar Park' from Ilkeston (Woodside) M.R.S., Peter Kazer's 'Corris', Murray Reid's 'Camp 4 at 3 Chop Ridge', 'Rothby' by Paul Windle, 'Kingston Regis' by John and Jane Jacobs, 'Eden Park and Dealms Valley Steam Railway' from E. and E. Farnell, 'Foxbury' by R. Brown and 'Belliver' by Steve Sims. Ian Futers brought 'Cold Harbour Lane', Peter Kibble brought 'Severn Mill', Mike Sharman brought 'Credibility Gap and Bottom End' and M. Lloyd brought 'Biggleswade'. John and Stella New had the 'Classic Train Set' and Peter Fletcher brought 'Ardbealach'. Alan Woodford exhibited 'Horselunges', whilst Chris Hewitt and the Liverpool M.R.S. showed 'Olive Mount Cutting'.

On the first floor mezzanine were; Ian Clarke's 'Rockingham Pottery', Andy Morris with 'Middleton Parkside', Bob Harper with 'Teign House Sidings', Rex Ashton with 'Bahnhof Konigsdorf', North Gwent Railway Modellers with 'Skenfrith' and Richard and Sue Andrews with 'Stanton Lacey'.

The first floor main level had 'Mickledore' from the Normanton club, 'Porthfedor and Abercoate' from Mike Gough, Mike Walshaw's 'Westport' and Gary Stone and Fenton Fouracre with 'Westford'. The second floor mezzanine had '14th Street Yard' from R. Taylor, 'Lutzen' from D. O'Rourke, 'Acton Mainline' from Croydon and District M.R.S. and 'Oxendale Junction' from the Wolverhampton club.

Society stands included; 009 Society, H.M.R.S., E.M.G.S., Scale Seven Group, 2mm Finescale Association, N Gauge Society, the 7mm Narrow Gauge Society and a display for the Warley National Exhibition. Preservation lines supporting were the North Yorkshire Moors, the East Lancashire and Isle of Man Railways. Demonstrators included Steve Banks, Geo. Norton, Peter Trigwell, Tony and Sue Hill, Derek Mundy and the Friends of South Devon.

(Photo courtesy Railway Modeller)

In 1988, Highland Railway days featured on Peter Fletcher's 'Ardbealach'.

(Photo courtesy Railway Modeller)

Also in 1988, Alan Woodford's unusual but entertaining 'Horselunges'.

the addition of Oldbury Models on their own instead of on a joint stand with Jim McGowen, Fox Transfers appeared for the first time as did David Geen, Four Track Models and Tower Models. Out, this year, went Comet (but returned the next), Wild Swan Publications, Timbercraft, Puffers, Model Railway Enthusiast, Video 125 and Eileen's Emporium (as it had changed hands). The York Engineers were with us for a last time.

Thus we began to 'settle in' in the new facilities. One thing which became evident very early in our use of the new stand was that layouts on the second floor mezzanine were just 'not on' - there wasn't enough room so we had to major, in future years, on that floor being mainly a trade area. We grew, in 1999 to the optimum size. There is more space but, with our resources and manpower, we just are not able to contemplate more. We feel that we would also lose the friendly atmosphere we have always been keen to maintain and what is more, we have already been accused of including too much! Each year we have a number of comments from folk that say, "There is too much to see in a day."

This year, we took over the whole of the ground floor, the first floor mezzanine and the main first floor, the second floor mezzanine and the main second floor. Once again York Banqueting supplied visitors' refreshment on the third floor. Attendance, this year, was another 100 up;

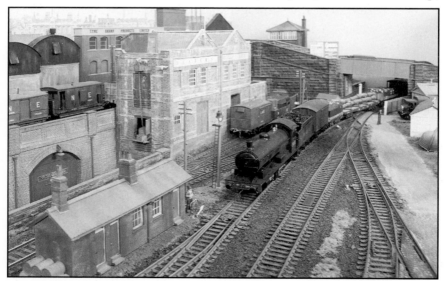

(Photo courtesy Railway Modeller)

Michael Thomas' wonderful LNER based layout 'Whitley South Dock' appeared at the 1999 show.

we were slowly beginning to draw back those who had left after the 'Trauma Year'. This year also saw a change of the treasurer; Joe Wills had been treasurer ever since The Friends of York Model Railway Show had been formed way back in the late 1960s and he had been an extremely good treasurer - one of the best. I was very worried as to what might happen but I managed to persuade John Shaw to take over (on the understanding that Joe and John would work closely together for the first year to ensure continuity). I had known John for a great number of years, he had joined my junior club as a young teenager and had, after a number of years, left to do his own thing. He returned onto the modelling scene as a very competent modeller and I had included several of his layouts in the Show over the past few years. I was confident that John would be able to do the job, but being the treasurer meant that he had, as I have had, to give up the idea of ever exhibiting one of his own layouts in the Show, at least for as long as he is in office. Joe had also to make this sacrifice, but soon made amends after his retirement!

In the trade department this year, we lost Oldbury Models (who had ceased trading), Wild Swan (who kept 'flying' in and 'flying' out) and Irwell Press. Both Comet and Eileen's Emporium were back, along with Procast, Freestone Modelling Accessories and Coopercraft/Mailcoach.

By this time we had an arrangement with Pullman Coaches of York who organised our regular bus service from the York Railway Station. This service had started when West Yorkshire Road Car Co. ran all the local services, and a good job they had made of it too. After deregulation the job was taken over by Rider York and things did not go quite as sweetly, matters coming to a head when we discovered, on the first day of the Show in 1997 that there was NO bus service from the railway station. We felt we had been severely let down and I told the firm this. Their answer was "take it or leave it," so I searched for another firm to do the job. As it turned out, the person in charge of the York Pullman Bus Co. was a modeller whom I had known for a great many years; he had also been in charge of the first of our bus services to the Racecourse back in 1991. We stayed with Pullman until they, too, were taken over in 1999. On consultation with my contact he advised that he would be starting his own business, but definitely not in time for the 2000 Show. He recommended us to book with Reliance Motor Services, with the proviso that we would look upon him kindly when he was up and running. Reliance were very good and, under normal circumstances, I would have continued with them, as it was, I had made a promise which I kept, and in 2001 the services between the railway station and the Racecourse were in the hands of Top Line Travel. Exhibits, in 1999 included, for the first time, some fine models made in 1/4 scale by our long-time electrician Benny Wood. This year Ben showed us a working signal which was displayed in the entrance foyer and was pulled off whenever the Show was open. Again appearing were most of the usual preservation and scale societies together with a number of demonstrators and static exhibits from the clubs and societies who assisted us. They were accompanied by forty one layouts.

1999

On the ground floor were; 'Brockholes' by Paul Gregory, 'Everingham' by Alan Smith, 'Herculaneum Dock' by Mike Edge, 'Middlepeak' by Geraint Hughes, 'Aidensfield Junction' by Whitby and District M.R.S., 'Calder Bridge' by the Newcastle and District M.R.C., 'West Bridgeford' by A. Knox, 'Chiseldon' by D. Barrett, 'New Bryford' by Mick Bryan, 'Broad Green' 3mm by Bruce Smeatham, 'East Clintwood' by Roger Nicholls, 'Neunberg' by our immediate past treasurer Joe Wills, 'Teignton Sands' by the Southend and District M.R.C., 'Rainton Colliery' by Jack Burnard, 'Chesil Exchange' by Mike Hayward, 'Stoke Fleming' by A. Searle, 'Tewkesbury Quay Branch' by the Orpington and District M.R.C., 'Semerdale' by Derek Naylor, 'Highworth' by S. Brasier, 'Isle of Man Railways' live steam by B. Caton, 'Penny Forum' by Leo McCarty, 'Ghylldale' by John Varley, 'Arcadia' by Martin Brent, 'Thunders Hill' by P. Bossom and 'Elmwell Village Depot' by B. Jerkins.

On the first floor mezzanine were; 'Broom Junction' from Warley M.R.C., 'Inver' from John Seward and 'Abbots Dale' from the Ely and District M.R.C. On the main first floor were; Chris Payne's 'St Pierre (canal) et la Rue Perrin', 'Overlord' from Chris Mead, 'Millbridge Sorting Sidings' from John Dillnott, 'Syreford Station' from Roger Brown, Richard and Sue Andrews with 'Thorne St. Margarets'. On the second floor were; 'Littlebeck' from Allen Grice and Andy Crawshaw, 'Millport Victoria' from Wigan M.R.S., Fraser Brown's 'Ardeval', 'Cranleigh Down' by Ian Saunders, 'Tavistock South' by Richard Simmons and Colin McCallum. Ken Gibbons from Hull M.R.S. exhibited 'Lapford Road', Chris Hewitt and the Liverpool lads with 'Swan Street Goods', The Model Railway Club returned with 'Copenhagen Fields' and that wonderful model from Michael Thomas, 'Whitley South Dock' completed the list.

The Millennium Show in 2000 was our tenth Show at the Racecourse. Already we were good friends with all the Racecourse staff with whom we had dealings but our relations could have been a great deal better with York Banqueting. True they supplied everything we required but 'at a price' and this year we had to stop the provision of a hot midday meal for all our exhibitors as the cost was escalating so much. We therefore decided to supply our exhibitors with tea and coffee and to establish an Exhibitors Rest Room on the first floor mezzanine. We also decided to provide exhibitors and stewards with a payment in lieu of a lunch. They could then spend this as they wished - either in goods before coming to the Show or at the official cafeteria on the third floor.

This year we had made contact with the National Railway Museum and had agreed that at least every other bus service would continue on from the Railway Station to the National Railway Museum. This, I fear, was a disaster and worked against the Show. Whilst they at the museum were almost 1000 up on attendance figures for no other explainable reason we were 885 down! We advertised the museum well at the Show and allowed the Friends to give out concessionary tickets for it. They had a

(Photo courtesy Railway Modeller)

Peter Kazer has exhibited at York for over twenty years and returned in 2000 with his Southwold Railway layout 'Blythburgh'.

2000

Modelling demonstrations in 2000 came from Steve Barnfield, George Norton, the Friends of South Devon, John Seward, Barry Norman, Martyn Welch, Bob and Gwen Dawson and Carl Legg. Society stands included; the 009 Society, 2mm Finescale Association, G.N.R. Society, Wolverhampton M.R.S., S7 Society, N.Y.M.R., H.M.R.S., N.E.R.A., R.C.T.S., East Lancashire R.P.S., N Gauge Society, and E.M.G.S. Mr Wigston had his usual railway art display.

Layouts in 2000 featured on the ground floor were; 'Sca Gill' from the Little Midland Society, David J. Haynes' 'Manx Electric Railway' (where the kids were encouraged to drive), Maurice Bramley's 'Bamburgh', 'Blythburgh' by Peter Kazer, 'Llansillin' by Rex Ashton, 'Walker Marine' Neil Ripley, Colin Stark and Malcolm Baker. 'Copperas Hill' by Phil Baggaley, Trevor Hughes' 'Tan Y Grisiau' (one of my, if not the, all time favourite layouts), 'Kennett' by Chris Clegg and Hughie Flynn, 'Kingswear' by Mervyn Seal, 'Dduallt' by D and R Waller, 'Narberth' by the Cardiff 4mm Group, 'Barrowfleet' of Hull M.R.S., 'Great Bardfield' by D. Hawkins, Mike Sharman's 'Early Railways', 'Beckley Tramway' by D. Medhurst, Tony Hill's 'Dursleyish - a Winter's Tale (and complete, on the last day, with falling snow!), 'The Far Twittering & Oysterperch' from Warley M.R.C., 'Smug Oak' from Watford M.R.C., 'Hammeston Wharf from the Macclesfield M.R.G. and 'Ashdan Sidings' from Barry Platt.

On the first floor mezzanine were; Chris Payne's 'Portpyn' and 'Leeds Trams and Middleton Parkside' from Andy Ross and Andy Morris. On the main first floor were; 'Forthal Schmalspurbahn' from Edinburgh and Lothians Club, 'Belton LNWR' from D. Martin and I. Harris, 'Croscombe' and 'Auchlin' in ScaleSeven and a partly built Irish broad and narrow gauge layout from John Seward who stood in, at the last minute, for a very ill Vic Halliwell.

The second floor featured 'Millers Dale' by David Smart of the Hull M.R.S., 'Starbeck Bridge' from the Leyland M.R.S., 'Steamboat Springs' from Don Annison, 'Thompson's End and 'tother end' by Malcolm Crawley, 'Tolcarn Engine Shed' by Terry Yeend, 'Ramsgate Harbour' by Peter Smith, 'Tan Y Coed' by Steve Flay, 'Calstock Quay' by Chris Peacock., 'St. George's Hill' by Ian Hopkins, 'Regent Road' by Chris Hewitt and Liverpool M.R.C., 'West Harptree' by Mike Corp and last but not least Ray and Cida Earl's 'Waterley Cross'.

prime site in the Show entrance; they loaned us the Crewe Works shunter 'Pet', but I fear they did little advertising for us in the museum.

Once again the Mammoth Gavioli was on display, with the preserved motor coaches but, this year, there was a problem. Had I known of this beforehand, I could have sorted it out but I had no idea until after the Show of what had happened. It seems that during the period between the 1999 and 2000 Shows the Racecourse had added a new outdoor security system to all of the areas around the new stand. If anyone moved within these areas the alarm system was triggered, not only in the home of the caretaker but also in the local police station. Nick Johnson had found it impossible to switch the security system on because of the Gavioli and its crew, plus the one or two other caravanning exhibitors (who, once again, I knew little of), occupying the area at night. Had I known of this I would, immediately, have asked those staying overnight within the area to find alternative sites for their vehicles; though in reality, it would not have been easy. Thus it was decided soon afterwards that we would have no outdoor exhibits in the immediate future years and until something could be sorted out.

Once again, Ben Wood brought along his 1/4 scale models; this year level crossing gates joined the signal. They were, because of the National Railway Museum stand, located in the ground floor main hall. Trade in 2000 saw the exit of both Crownline and Chowbent. Andy Duncan also felt, reluctantly, that he could not afford to continue. Newcomers this year were Picture Pride Displays.

It was after the Show closed, on the Tuesday night, that I was taken aside by my friend Owen and told some 'home truths' regarding what others on the committee were thinking, discussing and doubting. The main issue was that most thought I was, physically, doing too much; I should leave more of the actual running of the Show to the others and not take on such a hefty workload; they genuinely worried for my health. At the same time the traders at the Show were becoming a little apprehensive about the length of the Show. Four days were a little too long to sustain and they were finding it hard to cover their costs and keep their attendance at the Show viable. It was also brought to my notice about the outdoor security too. I had much to think about over the coming days; much to be a little upset over but a great deal to be thankful for.

It was gratifying to see the faces of the Friends at the first meeting after the Show. I had taken all their worries, all their problems and sorted them before the meeting! Yes, we would return to being a three day Show, yes

'Barrowfleet' visited York for a second time in 2000. The layout portrayed a small brickworks serviced by a narrow gauge railway, the disused parts of which had been adopted by a preservation society which ran services on Sundays for the public, seen here in this early view.

we would open 'regular' hours, yes I would take more of a back seat at the venue and trust others to do the jobs they had undertaken to do, and yes we wouldn't have the Mammoth Gavioli next year! (I had been pondering over this one myself for some time, anyhow). I have always been able to listen, and have learned, over the years not to always accept that my opinion is correct! I am sure that I'm just like most people who take pride in their aims and objectives, and find that it isn't always easy to accept when you are in the wrong.

So to the 39th Show in 2001. A few weeks before it took place the Foot and Mouth Epidemic broke out and it looked, at one time, as if the Show might have to be cancelled. Day by day, I watched to see if the outbreak was spreading into our area and, luckily, it remained at least 40 or more miles away.

This Show was held on the Saturday, Sunday and Monday only, from 10.00 am to 5.00 pm each day. One slight change was that in common with one or two other Shows, and in order to minimise the initial crush, advance booked tickets were admitted in 15 minutes beforehand. We were a little apprehensive that, because we had decided to open only on three days, we would find a reduction in attendance figures, however, to the contrary we were 755 up on the previous year. We occupied all the same areas in the stand as the previous year and overall, with few problems to

(Photo courtesy Railway Modeller)

Scarborough Central Station, modelled by members of the Scarborough and District M.R.C., appeared in the 2001 Show.

speak of, it proved to be a really excellent Show, and one which can do only good for our reputation in the future.

This year, Peter Dew was able to provide the bus service from the railway station and we were able to have a route which brought customers right up to the 'doorstep'. One difficulty however, was car parking, not because of foot and mouth, but because of the amount of rain all of Yorkshire had soaked up over the Winter. This had left the ground extremely waterlogged and meant that the Car Boot Sale which usually took place on the Saturday (our busiest day), could not take place allowing us to have the 'through route' for our bus service. Car parking was going to be difficult, though, but as it turned out John Weston and Peter Kibble, our stewards in charge, did not have too many problems and only a few 'tow-outs' were required.

This was the year when I did what I had been asked to do; take more of a back seat during the Show. Bachmann had provided us with a new information stand and I asked Gareth Coles to take charge of it. He, instead of I, would deal with all the visitor queries and make all the public address announcements. He would be assisted by at least two others, leaving me, I thought, free to 'make my rounds', do a bit of demonstrating and a bit of

Two modellers whose connections with York Show go back over 30 years are Neil Rushby and Bob Dawson. In 2001, Neil, together with Alan Price, exhibited 'Outwell Village' (opposite) and Bob and his wife Gwen brought 'Aber-wryst-watch' (above). (Photos courtesy Railway Modeller)

2001

Starting on the left hand side of the ground floor we had 'Rhydypenau Light Railway' from Tony Bird of Cardiff, Ian Futers' latest offering 'Percy Street' and Peter Kirmond's ScaleSeven project 'Brill'. Other layouts here were 'Acton Lane' by P.Clarke, 'Holmehurst' by K. Lodge, 'Glyn Mawr by Derek Mundy, 'Bullmoose' by Phil Baggaley, 'Hellingley Hospital Railway' by Phillip Parker, 'Hallbury' - Vic Halliwell's layout a year later than it should have been, and 'Angel Bank' by Chris Hewitt and the Liverpool M.R.S.

In the corridor between the two areas on the ground floor were; 'Scarborough Central' from Scarborough and District M.R.C., 'Iron Mould Lane' by R.S. Lear and 'Sheepwash' by Ken Gibbons.

In the other part of the ground floor were; 'Orton in Dabble' by Richard Chapman, 'Zertrummelt' by Steve Pugmire of Hull M.R.S., 'Peakdale' from the Lincoln and District M.R.S., 'Littlewood' by Richard and Christine Deas and Gary Atkinson, 'Ashcross Industrial Museum' by Robin Edwards, 'Ty Mawr' by Paul Towers, 'Aber-Wryst-Watch by Bob and Gwen Dawson, 'Darenth Junction' by Ivan Maxted, 'Sellindge' by John Smith, 'Sheffield Bridgehouses 1845' by John Quick and 'Outwell Village' by Neil Rushby and Alan Price.

On the first floor mezzanine were; 'Pilot Bridge' by Farnham and District M.R.C., 'Water Street Yard' by Paul Smith and 'Upper Hill' from the North Gwent Railway Modellers. On the main first floor proper; 'Crystal Lake (Oregon)' from Roger Nicholls, 'Milford' by Tony Kell, 'Tan Yr Allt' by Roger Christian, 'Pagham Harbour' by Richard Glover, 'Ditton Railway Company' by John Thorne, 'Llanfair' by John Coulter and 'Federal Street Yard' by John H. Wright.

Layouts on the second floor came from Alan Lawrence with 'Shipden', Tony Sims 'Masham' and from abroad, Otto Schouwstra's 'Eneret'. Also on the second floor were 'Pratts Sidings' by R. and M. Clarke, 'West Park' by Hull M.R.S., 'Eastwell Ironstone Company' from Greg Brooks, Paul James and friends, 'Briding Noora' - a layout using an ironing board as a frame, by Peter Leadley, 'Minsterley' by Peter Gentle, 'Chevineaux le Grande' by R. Pooley and C. Richards, 'Eden Valley' from the Glaxo M.R.S. and last but certainly not least 'Thomas the Tank Engine' from Warley Model Railway Club.

chatting, but still be there in a Chairman/Show Manager capacity, if needed to make the ultimate decisions if necessary.

It didn't work out completely like that - it never does - but I did have a far more relaxed Show than I have ever had previously. Just as well, for I had been 'under the weather' for over five months before the Show and took at least two weeks to recover afterwards.

The wonderful aspect in 2001 was the atmosphere amongst the exhibitors; everyone was happy and worked together as a team. There was no back-biting, no talking in cliques, everyone had a smile on their face and was enjoying the experience. For me this was personally gratifying, after almost forty years, with major upheavals every few years, clashes with folk over policy issues and all sorts of management problems, my vision of the perfect York Model Railway Show was at last in my grasp.

There were still several changes though; John Lundie returned to assist the treasurer, and Joe Wills (who had taken over again for a three month stint whilst John Shaw had been in Italy) also helped in the treasury. We did away with the assistance from St. John Ambulance this year, they had been undependable the year before and as we had several trained and certificated medics amongst our stewards and exhibitors who were willing to do the job, we depended on them instead. John Russell took over as chief steward for the whole of the building we used, whilst Dick Dring returned to his first love - exhibitors refreshments and rest room, although he continued to do the steward rostering. Bernard Davies has found a niche for himself; York Show Guide sales, assisted by wives of Friends of South Devon which I enlisted. As I said earlier, there was nothing placed out of doors on Show this year. Benny Wood's signalling models greeting folk first as they entered the building and on the floor was another 'experiment'. As stated previously, folk like Andy Duncan could not afford to bring a full sales stand to the Show and I regretted that products such as his, and also those which Jim Harris produces, should be unavailable because of this. I therefore devised a stand where the persons in question would do modelling demonstrations, but also have items from their range available. Carl Legg had already done this the year before. The stands were nominated as 'Doing a Duncan' and 'Doing a Harris' and seemed to work very well.

Finally, in 2001 for the first time in the show's 39 year history I included a layout from abroad; Otto Schouwstra's 'Eneret'- which, with its special sound effects, captivated our visitors. Society stands and demonstrators were very much as usual this year with one or two additions, whilst the trade stayed much the same as in past years, although there was one

(Photo courtesy Continental Modeller)

York Show's first overseas exhibit, 'Eneret' captivated the public in 2001.

'leaver' - Coopercraft. Ian Kirk and C & L Finescale joined the gang for the first time.

So... this brings me up to the present day and contemplating the future. Yes, there will be a future and, I hope, for many years to come. I am coolly confident that, although I may not be able to be so active during the Show, there will be many more which I can organise. Trusting that my health stays well enough for me to do so, I have often said to others, and I certainly mean it with conviction, that I wish to be 'in harness' for the 50th Show; then I might just see about taking things a little quieter! The truth is, I thrive on the work for the Show and get very low when there's nothing to do. It has taken over a great deal of my time, perhaps even my life, especially since we moved into the new stand. For example, posting a notice to all the exhibitors means somewhere in the region of 130 letters have to be produced, and that's just for a start! Perhaps, someday, I might find a little time to do some modelling - I currently get most of that done at other folks' exhibitions - but I can't build the layout itself there!

Yes, this is only a break in a continuing narrative; look out for the next instalment...

Postscript

So You Want to Exhibit Your Layout?

It has been suggested that it might be a good way to complete this 'epic' of mine by recounting how layouts get invited to the York Model Railway Show. In other words, the process I use to select the layouts for inclusion in the show, so this I shall now attempt.

Firstly, there are no hard and fast rules for this. However, I generally don't like folk to thrust details of their layouts at me. In the past when this has happened I have usually found the layouts to be over-enthused somewhat by their owners and not really all that good for public display.

A great deal is left to my own intuition and experience but also, I depend, to some extent at least, on the support and recommendations of several of my modelling friends who come from all over the United Kingdom. These people, who have become my friends over a period of many years, have been asked by myself to look out for anything which would be an asset at the York Show. Often during conversation, they will mention a layout or layouts and, in most cases, will have obtained details on paper to substantiate their recommendation. Occasionally, I have to be cautious here too, as their suggestions can be a little too biased towards their own specific interest, but I feel that, nowadays, I have enough experience to realise when this is the case and it definitely is not the norm, I can assure you.

Really, to be absolutely sure of a layout, I must have photographic evidence at least. Better still, I should actually have seen the layout myself and seen it working. This I try and stick too, as I have learned to my cost in the past that sometimes when a layout, photographically, looks superb - well detailed and beautifully executed - it can run 'like a bag of old nails'.

Thus, for a layout from an unknown source I should have had at least an enthusiastic recommendation from a colleague, whom I really trust, or I should have seen the layout myself at another exhibition. In the latter situation I will obtain the details or sometimes even invite them on the spot.

For those layout builders who are well known on the 'circuit' and have an established 'track record' (pun not intended!), I can usually accept their layouts without initial vetting. This is generally the case with those individuals or groups who have been regular exhibitors at York for many years. I'm often accused of only inviting my 'close circle of friends' to exhibit at York; this is not the case. Although they certainly are friends of mine, they are invited regularly because I know, and trust, that they can 'deliver the goods' (again, pun not intended!) and bring a layout that is worthy of display. There have been very few times when I have been proved wrong in this 'department'.

So, how do you get 'on the circuit' in the first place? Well the best way is either by initially joining a modelling club or a scale society or association (such as the EMGS or N Gauge Society), or by having your layout accepted for publication in one of the major modelling magazines. If you take the former course you can offer your own layout for inclusion in the society's own annual exhibition. This will give your peers and the public the opportunity to view and experience your efforts and, if it is genuine 'exhibition material' then you'll soon be spotted and invited to 'guest' at other exhibitions. At the same time, you will soon learn from your fellow members what your shortcomings are and, if it is anything of a club at all, will be pointed in the right direction and assisted to improve in those quarters. If you are invited to exhibit as a guest exhibitor, your efforts will soon get noticed by other exhibition managers further afield. I am always on the lookout for new and interesting exhibits to 'ring the changes' and provide something fresh at our event. I am sure other exhibition managers do the same too, so it shouldn't be long before you are invited to other shows.

Having been invited to an exhibition once, don't assume you will be invited back the following year with the same layout, this will only happen if you have made drastic changes or additions. Show managers don't generally like to include the same model year-on-year unless, there is some specific reason for so doing. However, if you have a reputation for building something new each year then you may get invited for the following year.

A word of caution; don't accept every invitation you are given, be selective, especially time-wise, as it is all too easy to find yourself out every weekend, or every other weekend, during the main 'season' and this can soon pall. I know of several excellent modellers who wore themselves out by doing this, and are now no longer interested in either exhibiting or modelling!

With my latest layout I have decided, because of my age and infirmities, etc., to exhibit only once every three months; this decision has the added advantage that the exhibition 'life' of the layout is prolonged (i.e. it doesn't become over-exposed), and, what's more, I also gain the time in between shows, to work on a new project which will replace the present one when it does eventually become time-expired.

What kind of a layout is most likely to be invited to the York Show? This one is difficult to answer, but whatever it is, it must have certain qualities that make it entertaining and interesting and able to meet the expectations of the visiting public. Essentially, it must be modelled to a competent standard and operate with the absolute minimum of derailments and 'finger poking'. Given those qualities, the other factors, to be quite honest, really depend on what I've already planned to include and what else I will need in order to give a good overall representation of our hobby. I always try to include as wide a range of scale and gauge combinations as possible, from the smallest up to the largest acceptable indoors. Usually it extends from either Z Gauge, or 2mm Finescale, up to 7mm, sometimes to Gauge 1 or G Scale. At the same time I have to provide both continuous running and end-to-end style layouts, equally represented, if possible. Overall not an easy task considering all the other factors involved. So it is that I am often 'accused' of bias; towards end-to-end branch termini, towards a specific scale/gauge, towards a specific company, or whatever. No exhibition manager is infallible, he can only provide what is available to him, so, really an exhibition manager's lot is not necessarily a happy one! - placing himself in a position to be 'shot at', often by visitors who are rather biased themselves!

My only answer is that I try to do my best. It is much the same for all show managers; it really is a labour of love with nothing in recompense for your efforts other than the knowledge that you've tried your hardest and that you have managed to entertain a sizeable proportion of the public.

So in addition to the above, is there anything otherwise which influences my choice of layouts? Definitely, yes! These include; physical size, the cost of bringing it to York and the number of operators it requires.

When I invite a layout to a Show I always ask the owner(s), in the first instance, several most important questions; these require written answers on an Exhibitor's Reply Sheet. The questions have become necessary through my years of experience and there are several for which I MUST have correct answers before I finally agree to the layout's appearance:

1) The overall space required and the layout's actual size; this has evolved recently through some exhibitors' erring on the side of caution and advising me of a much larger area requirement than was actually needed - thus leaving large areas of unused space which could have otherwise been filled with exhibits. It is most important, and I have always attempted, to give visitors the best value for their entrance fee and to see too much empty space, as with past Shows on occasions has disappointed me.

2) Transportation costs. Exhibitors usually arrange their own van hire, or use of private cars, and we reimburse all transport and travelling expenses. As I have had great experience with this myself over the years, I am aware of the costs incurred and can easily spot anyone who is not being completely genuine with their requests, perhaps also adding sums, on the side, to pay towards extra meals, beer money and so forth! I do always tell them that we only pay for van hire and fuel costs and that anything else MUST be stated. We still get greatly overestimated expenses sometimes, but these are quickly weeded out. We then contact them again and ask for a breakdown of their estimate, unless we are satisfied with their reply their invitation is subsequently withdraw; fortunately this hasn't happened very often.

3) Number of operating positions on the layout. I ask this because it is important that layouts are not over-staffed, or worse still, used as a means of getting a cheap trip to York! Sometimes this situation can occur when the layout comes from a group within a club, perhaps unintentionally, but 'the more' is not necessarily 'the merrier' in this case. We generally allow for up to two persons for each operating position (one on duty, one off) but are happy if the owners can cope with less. This is all because the fewer the folk, then the fewer the number of bed spaces needed, the smaller number of cars requiring fuel costs reimbursements and the fewer quantity of meal allowances to pay out.

York Show, like any other exhibition, has escalating costs; none more so than with the accommodation of exhibitors. Costs per person per night have risen greatly over the past few years and, unlike other exhibitions, we are generally not able to organise special rates as the show takes place over a Bank Holiday weekend. Accommodation is our largest single expense; far greater than any other.

It's not that we are miserly about costs, but they all have to be recouped through admission fees, and if our aim is to give value for money, then costs must be kept down. I'm sure our visitors, who are our 'customers' of course, would be most unhappy if they thought that they were paying for 'junkets'.

Thus, prospective exhibitors need to be aware that they should be completely straightforward and honest in their information. This is one of the ways they will attain a 'good name' amongst exhibition managers; for, believe me, exhibition managers do talk to one another and individual exhibitors are often discussed, especially those who may not have been completely honest in their dealings. I need to add here, that those who are always fair are noted too!

So, in conclusion, may I say to all those 'foolhardy' enough to want to build a layout for exhibition purposes; and perhaps bring it along the York Show, you will increase your chances of being accepted if;

- Your layout runs efficiently.
- Your layout is scenically good.
- Your layout has been accepted by your peers as being entertaining to the public.
- You play fair with out of pocket expenses, numbers of operators, etc.

You will probably find it jolly hard work, but the rewards are well worth it. Above all, you will receive the acceptance and appreciation of the visiting public and experience the camaraderie of your fellow exhibitors. You will also need stamina; there's no doubt about that. Keeping the trains running all the time can be tiring and the 'apres show' activities will take even more out of you.

Although we do set high standards, as do most other shows, they are attainable by all competent modellers. Don't be downhearted if you're not accepted onto the 'circuit' straightway, it can take time, and often shows are booked up two years in advance. And do not be put off by what I term the 'higher echelons' of the modelling fraternity; as with all hobbies we do have our quota of those self-appointed experts who look down their noses at anyone not reaching their required standards. I say to those types that they should remember railway modelling is a hobby practised for enjoyment within which there are many levels of achievement; *all* of which are just as important as the others.

I will end this postscript with my well known comment:

"We're modellers because we enjoy modelling and can appreciate the work of others, whatever the standard. If modelling ever stops being enjoyable and we stop appreciating the work of others, then we should get out of the hobby straightway - and take up fishing... or something!"

So goodbye for now, and happy modelling!

Heartiest Congratulations
from
PECO PUBLICATIONS
to Mike Cook on his 40th York Model Railway Exhibition

RAILWAY MODELLER
The essential monthly magazine for all railway enthusiasts

CONTINENTAL MODELLER
Monthly coverage for those interested in overseas railways everywhere

PECO PUBLICATIONS & PUBLICITY LTD
Beer · Seaton · Devon · EX12 3NA

Other titles available from Santona Publications

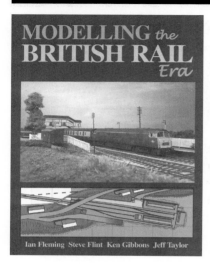

Other titles available from Santona Publications

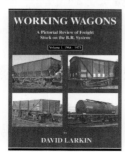

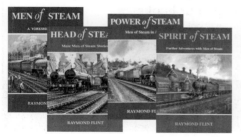

Acknowledgements

The author and publishers would like to thank Peco Publications and Publicity Ltd. for their cooperation and support in the preparation of this book. Photographs, unless otherwise credited, are from the collections of Mike Cook and Steve Flint, and appear courtesy of Brian Monaghan, Barry Norman, Railway Modeller, Continental Modeller and the Yorkshire Evening Press. Artwork courtesy of the City of York Tourism Department and Baz Ward.